Build It.
Fix It.
Make It Work.

the set-up Workbook *for* Law Firms

Simone Fulmer Gaus

PAGE TWO

Cataloguing in publication information
is available from Library and Archives Canada.
ISBN 978-1-77458-803-1 (paperback)

Page Two
pagetwo.com

Cover, interior design, and illustrations by Fiona Lee

theset-up.co

Contents

Let's Get You Set Up

HELLO AND WELCOME! I'm so glad you're here. Truly. The fact you picked up this workbook says a lot: You've decided the way things are isn't the way they have to stay. You care enough about your firm—and yourself—to do something different and take your firm where you've always wanted it to be. That's huge.

But any work you do on your firm only matters if you're clear on what you're working toward. What do you really want from your firm?

- Do you want freedom—to know the work will keep moving even when you're not there?
- Do you want peace of mind—to leave the office at night without carrying it all home in your head?
- Do you want a team you can trust—people who take ownership instead of waiting on you for every answer?
- Do you want clarity and control—not over every little detail, but over the noise, so you can finally focus on what matters?
- Do you want true profitability—growth that shows up in your bank account, not just on your to-do list?

Whatever your answer, hold it close. Because that's what you're working toward, your *why*. Write it down here. (Really, write it down. One day you'll come back to it and be amazed at all you've accomplished.)

My *why*? The thing that led me to create everything you'll find in this workbook? It's that I wanted a self-managing firm. I wanted an approach to the practice of law that would sustain my team *and* me. I wanted to stop carrying the firm home every night. I wanted a team that could think, decide, and act without me holding it all together. I wanted a firm that made money!

And, no, I didn't wake up one morning with it figured out. Not at all. I had to wrestle my way there. Because running a firm is hard. You're managing personalities, holding space for clients at their worst moments, and trying to keep your own energy from running dry while you struggle to keep the lights on. I stumbled plenty. I got things wrong. I fixed, re-fixed, and started again. But each stumble taught me something. And over time, I began to see patterns: where our struggles were coming from and what it really took to fix them. From that came the structure—the system—that changed everything. The Set-Up.

The Set-Up

What I found is that when you strip away all the noise that is "running a law firm," everything really falls into the same few categories, or pillars:

People: your culture, leadership, and values in action.

Pipeline: the clear path every case follows, with ownership at every stage.

Process: the how-tos that keep standards consistent and work moving.

Product: the legal services you deliver and the experience that sets you apart.

Profitability: the numbers, habits, and decisions that keep the firm healthy.

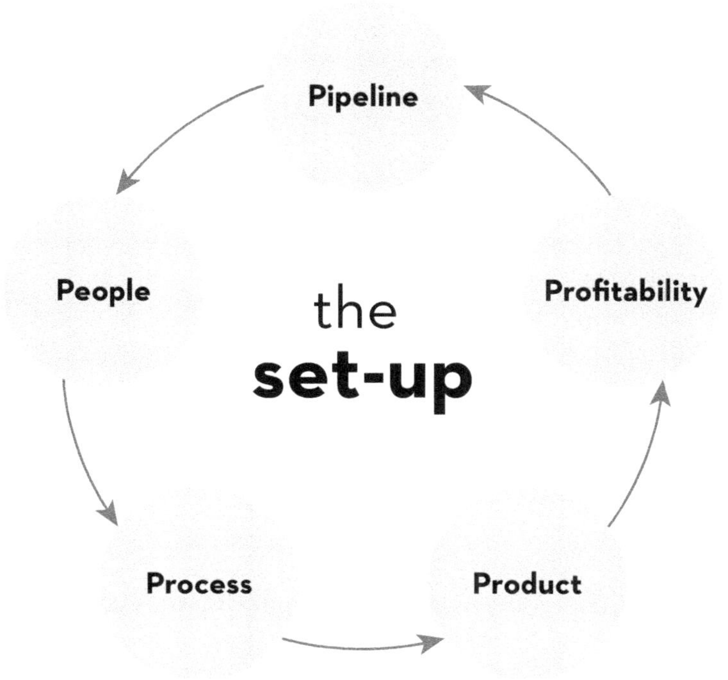

Each pillar naturally flows into the next. People bring values and leadership that drive the Pipeline forward. The Pipeline sets the stage for clear processes, or Process. Those processes protect the quality of the Product. And strong Product delivery fuels Profitability, which in turn supports our People.

Now, most days are like the one I had today, where Andrea already has the solution before I've even named the problem. Where Shelley works with the team to tweak our medical records process, and suddenly everyone's on the same page and saving hours of work a week. Where Chad celebrates a recent win in our Third Monday meeting, crediting Pipeline and Process for making our Product more predictable and our days less hectic. And where Lauren and Harrison dig into a Stage Three issue and resolve it without me having to steer.

Oh, and this is just Monday!

The very things I longed for—clarity, ownership, relief—are now woven into how my firm works. Eleven years since our start, our revenue is more than thirteen times what it was, and it's still climbing. And the best part is we got here without losing ourselves in the process.

This is what happens when you focus on your foundation. And it's what led me to write my book *The Set-Up*. It's for law firm owners and leaders like you who lie awake at night turning over culture problems, money worries, and the bone-deep exhaustion of carrying more than your share, wondering if this is simply the price of running a firm. (It doesn't have to be!)

This workbook is the book's practical companion. It's the hands-on, get-in-there-and-build-it space, where the concepts from the book turn into the structure your firm runs on. It's where you'll build and strengthen your pillars, work through challenges as they come up, and plan the moves that will take your firm where you want it to go.

No, you don't have to read the book to use this workbook, but I really wish you would. The book gives you the deeper context and the why behind everything we're building here. And the why matters: Without it, these exercises are just tasks you're checking off. With it, you'll understand what you're building and why each piece matters. That's when the work becomes the foundation that changes everything.

Working with This Workbook

Maybe you're building your firm from the ground up and don't have systems in place yet. Maybe you've been running it for years but can't figure out why things keep stalling. Maybe the concepts in the book resonated, but you're not sure which pillar to tackle first. No matter where you're starting from, this workbook is designed to meet you there. We'll build what's missing, solve what's stuck, and create a system that works.

Think of this workbook as your ongoing Set-Up strategy. It's not meant to be something you use once and shelve. And you don't need to sit down and fill it out front to back. In fact, I don't recommend it. You're not putting together an IKEA desk, after all. Your firm is just too important for that.

But before you dive into the pillars, you'll run The Set-Up Systems Check—a diagnostic tool that will show you which pillar needs attention first. It takes the guesswork out of where to start and gives you a baseline to measure your progress over time.

From there, the workbook is built around a similar structure as *The Set-Up* itself—chapters covering Pipeline, People, Process, Product, and Profitability. (We start with Pipeline because it's the framework that supports everything else.) Think of these as your "Build It" chapters. As you complete exercises for one pillar, you'll return to The Set-Up Systems Check to see where to focus next. This way, you'll create a foundation solid enough to support everything your firm does. You'll come back to these chapters often. Sometimes to build. Sometimes to rebuild. Sometimes just to tighten one loose screw.

And when something's not working, but you're not sure why, the "Fix It" chapter will show you how to trace the problem to its source. The pillars are interconnected—what looks like a People problem might actually be a broken Pipeline, or what feels like a Process failure might really be a Product misalignment. The "Fix It" chapter will help you find where the real problem lives.

In the "Make It Work" chapter, you'll find templates for The Set-Up Annual Plan and The Set-Up Quarterly Plan. These two tools are for capturing your goals, action steps, and timelines as you build and maintain your Set-Up. Using them ensures your firm works the way you've always wanted it to. As you go through the workbook, be on the lookout for those times I prompt you to record your Set-Up tasks and goals in one of your Set-Up plans.

And keep your workbook close. Mark it up. Dog-ear the pages. Use it with your team. (Maybe even get them their own copies!) Let it become the tool you reach for again and again as your firm grows, shifts, and steps into its next chapter.

How Much Time Will It Take?

Getting your firm where you want it to be will take time. I won't sugarcoat it. So, give yourself a little grace along the way. Rome wasn't built in a day, and neither is the firm that runs itself. My hope is you'll start to see the difference in your firm after a few small wins.

That said, you don't need to spend all day, every day working on your business. The best practice is to spend about 10 percent of your workweek. That's roughly four hours in a forty-hour week. And to be clear, it's not that 10 percent is the magic number. It's that, unless you give yourself time to work *on* your firm, everything stays stuck in the cycle of working *in* it. Gary Pisano notes in his article "Reflecting on Work Improves Job Performance" that even a modest investment of time in planning and reflection pays off in sharper performance and lower stress.

Now, if 10 percent of your workweek seems out of reach right now, start smaller. Carve out one hour a week and build from there. The key isn't the number; it's the *habit* you build. A consistent rhythm, even if it's just a sliver of your week, creates a space where real change can take hold.

So, decide ahead of time *when and where* that will happen. Maybe you block Friday afternoons after court. Maybe you set aside Monday mornings after your team huddle. This way, you're tying it to something you already do every week—a technique author James Clear calls "habit stacking" in his book *Atomic Habits*.

Just don't wait until you miraculously have time. You won't. You have to *make* it. Block it. Protect it. Call this your "Set-Up Time." Tell your team and your calendar to leave you alone while you focus on the business. And trust that your Set-Up Time (no matter how long you set aside) will become the lever for every other hour of your week.

One other thought—maybe the most important for some of us—often, we are far more reliable when someone else knows what we've committed to. When you ask someone to check in—whether it's a colleague, your assistant, or even your whole team—you raise the stakes. That little bit of social pressure is often just the nudge we need to stay consistent.

Set Your Set-Up Time Commitment

I commit to set aside

this much time: ______________________________

on this day each week: ______________________________

at this time: ______________________________

To keep me honest, I will put my Set-Up Time on the firm's calendar as a real appointment and ask ______________ to check in.

In this block, I'll work only on my firm, not in it.

Signed: ______________________________

The Set-Up Systems Check

"Which pillar should I start with?" is one of the most common questions I hear about implementing The Set-Up. And, like any good lawyer, I answer: "It depends."

We're all starting from different places. Some firms have their processes nailed down but a culture that's quietly fraying. Others have a solid team but no reliable way to keep cases moving. If we all line up at the same starting block, half of us would waste time fixing what isn't even broken while the real problem keeps bleeding energy and resources.

That's why I created The Set-Up Systems Check. It's like taking an X-ray of your firm so you can see what's really happening beneath the surface. This way, you'll know exactly where your energy is needed most. You can return to this Systems Check any time things feel off, when you're scaling, or after a big change. I also recommend you run the Systems Check quarterly as maintenance to keep your Set-Up healthy.

FOR EACH statement below, rate yourself honestly. Not where you wish you were, but where you actually are right now. You can do this on your own, with your partners, or bring in your team if you want a fuller picture.

Rating Scale

3 = Rock Solid: We can rely on this every time.
2 = Patchy: Here, but not dependable.
1 = Barely There: More of a hope than a habit.
0 = Missing: We don't have this yet.

People

____ 1. Our mission and values are clear and guide daily decisions.

____ 2. Leadership is steady, not reactive.

____ 3. Feedback is treated as a gift, not a threat, regardless of who's giving it.

____ 4. Culture feels respectful and psychologically safe.

____ 5. We address difficult issues early and do not avoid them.

____ 6. We hold each other accountable to our values.

Pipeline

____ 1. We have a clear path that every case follows from start to finish.

____ 2. The whole team understands what needs to happen to move a case along.

____ 3. Every task that needs to happen has someone responsible for getting it done.

____ 4. Anyone on the team can check where a case stands without needing to ask.

____ 5. We can spot slowdowns or stuck cases quickly and fix them early.

____ 6. Cases don't stall, waiting for one person to say what happens next.

Process

____ 1. The team can do routine work without constantly asking how.

____ 2. Everyone does the same task the same way.

____ 3. New hires are trained with step-by-step guidance, not just shadowing.

____ 4. Others can step in when someone is out.

____ 5. We've solved recurring problems instead of just working around them.

____ 6. Important knowledge doesn't walk out the door when people leave.

Product

____ 1. We have clear criteria for which cases we take and which we turn down.

____ 2. We know what each unique client really needs beyond just winning their case.

____ 3. What matters to the client shapes how we handle their case.

____ 4. Our team approaches similar cases the same way, no matter who's handling the case.

____ 5. Clients don't feel forgotten or left in the dark.

____ 6. Case strategy happens early, not as an afterthought.

Profitability

____ 1. We know the minimum monthly income needed to cover our firm's basic expenses.

____ 2. We can see cash crunches coming before they hit.

____ 3. We have a clear plan for what happens when money arrives (not just paying whatever's urgent).

____ 4. We have money set aside for slow months or emergencies.

____ 5. We track a few key numbers that show how the firm is performing overall.

____ 6. I pay myself consistently, and the firm can sustain that over time.

Scoring

People	____ /18
Pipeline	____ /18
Process	____ /18
Product	____ /18
Profitability	____ /18

Score Ranges (per pillar)

0–8 = Focus Here First: This pillar needs immediate attention.
9–13 = Stabilize: You've got a base, but it's wobbly. Tighten it before chasing new goals.
14–18 = Leverage: This is a strength. Use it to support weaker pillars.

What to Do Next

Your Systems Check shows which pillar needs attention first. Start by turning to that chapter and working through the exercises in it. If more than one pillar scored 0–8, start with Pipeline—it's the framework for everything else—or choose the pillar causing you the most stress right now. Just don't try to fix everything at once. Let each change settle before moving on. Real change takes root when it's given room to grow.

Use the space below to set a focus for ninety days. (And if your goal doesn't need the full ninety days, that's fine. Adjust the timeline to fit what you're building.) For example:

Pipeline scored 6/18 → Goal: Complete Pipeline Exercise 1 by March 15th, using my weekly Set-Up Time.

My Commitment

My focus this quarter (pick one pillar): ______________________

Date: ______________________

My SMART (specific, measurable, achievable, relevant, time bound) goal(s) for this pillar:

____

____

____

____

____

____

____

____

Record your commitment in your Set-Up Quarterly Plan.

When You're Just Starting Out

This is the system I wish I'd had when I started. It took me years of trial and error to piece it together. My hope is that finding The Set-Up early in your journey will spare you some of the hazards (and a lot of the headaches) that come with building a law firm from the ground up.

It does assume, though, that you're past the "hanging your shingle" phase and already have most of the basics in motion. So, here's a quick checklist to help you know if you're ready for The Set-Up. You don't have to check them all off, but if most are done—or you have a clear plan to complete them—you're good to go.

Is My Firm Ready for The Set-Up?

Legal & Business Foundations

☐ Bar admission and licensing completed.

☐ State business registration filed.

☐ Malpractice insurance secured.

☐ Partnership agreement reviewed by a lawyer and signed. *(Do this if you have a partner. You may think you and your best bud from law school can work it all out, but I've seen too many good firms—and relationships—come undone because they skipped this step.)*

Financial Systems

☐ Operating account opened.

☐ IOLTA (client trust account) opened.

☐ Bookkeeping software chosen and installed. *(Don't overthink this; just pick one and use it. A system you keep up with is better than the "perfect" one you never open.)*

☐ Accountant hired. *(And I don't just mean a tax preparer you see once a year. You need someone who understands law firm finances and gives you quarterly reports so you can make decisions with real numbers instead of guesses.)*

Start-Up Capital

☐ Personal savings, partner capital, or other financing source earmarked for start-up costs.

☐ Line of credit established before you need it. *(It's much easier to get when you're not desperate.)*

☐ Clear plan drawn up for how you'll cover payroll, rent, and insurance in the early months, when revenue is unpredictable.

Note: There are lenders who understand legal practices, and they can be a good fit. But don't overlook your local bank. Sometimes that relationship ends up being just as valuable when you need flexibility down the road.

Docketing & Calendaring (Critical)

☐ Firm-wide calendar/docket set up (no individual inbox calendars).

☐ Deadlines based on court rules for each jurisdiction calculated.

☐ Clear procedure for entering, verifying, and reviewing dates established (with whoever's responsible).

Tech & Operations

☐ Cloud vs. local server decision made.

☐ Case management software selected (or a plan for selecting one). *(I've run a firm with and without one. Trust me. If you're going to splurge anywhere, let it be here. It'll save you endless hours and might even save you from putting another salary on the books.)*

☐ Legal research system chosen. *(You don't need a Cadillac here, but you do need something. Pick a platform that fits your practice and your budget. You'll thank yourself when you're not scrambling for answers at midnight.)*

☐ Printer, scanner, and phone systems put in place.

Visibility & Communication

- ☐ Basic professional website launched.
- ☐ Clear description of practice areas and who you help posted.
- ☐ Email, voicemail, and intake systems working.

And don't forget, you don't have to figure all of this out on your own. Your state bar association and the American Bar Association both offer resources, checklists, and practice management guidance for new firms.

pipeline
your framework

MOST LAW FIRMS run on what I call "hallway management." It's where everything important happens in doorways and during passing conversations, somewhere between your office and the coffee machine. "Hey, what's next on the *Johnson* case?" "Did we file that motion?" "Where are we on discovery?"

You might think this is just how law firms work. You're managing complex cases with moving parts and tight deadlines. A little back-and-forth is normal, right? But those conversations have a way of becoming more than just casual check-ins. They morph into the only way information moves through your firm.

There's a reason for that.

The traditional law firm is built like a pyramid with you at the top. Every decision flows up and waits for your input because you've become the bottleneck, the nervous system of the whole operation. That might make you feel indispensable, but it's trapping you in the weeds when you should be running your firm.

And it's why those hallway conversations never stop. Your team can't move cases forward because they don't see the big picture. They don't know what comes next. So, they ask you. Again, and again. Every "where are we on this?" is time stolen from the strategic work only you can do. What you need is to reimagine the system itself. What you need is a Pipeline.

The Pipeline is the framework that defines how cases flow through your firm—from the first phone call to the closed file. You break down the journey the typical client case takes through your firm into stages, list specific tasks (what I call "Objectives") in each stage, and assign clear responsibility for who does what and when. With the Pipeline, your team sees where every case stands and what comes next without asking you.

Need a Refresher?

Go back to *The Set-Up*:

Chapter 3: A New Way to Work the Work, if you need a reminder of how the Pipeline breaks the case journey into clear stages, assigns ownership, and turns the unspoken swirl of tasks into something everyone can see.

Chapter 4: What Happens When the Work Works, if you need a reminder of how that structure provides smoother teamwork, real accountability, fewer bottlenecks, and a clearer picture of what's driving (or dragging down) your results.

Pipeline Exercise 1. Build Your Pipeline

To build your Pipeline, we'll take how cases actually move through your firm and turn that into a structure your whole team can see and follow.

You can do this alone, but I recommend you gather your key players—those who actually handle cases day-to-day. Whether it's your whole team or just a core group, input from people who do the work makes your Pipeline stronger and implementation smoother. Plus, when people help build the system, they're far more likely to use it.

You can do this during your Set-Up Time over a few weeks or in an afternoon or two to tackle it all at once. Yes, this takes time up front, but it will save you countless hours of repeated instructions later.

Here's a simple example of what we're going for. To see examples of the Pipeline for different practice areas, visit theset-up.co/workbookresources.

Sample Pipeline Stages and Objectives: Personal Injury Litigation Firm

	Intake	Stage One	Stage Two	Stage Three	Stage Four
	First Call → Contract Signed	Contract → Suit Filed/Settled	Filing → Resolution/Appeal	Resolution → Distribution	Final Appealable Order → Resolution
Objectives	• Gather information & documents • Meet with client • Decide to accept or decline • Execute attorney-client agreement • Docket statutes of limitation • Send Client Welcome Packet	• Continue to gather evidence • Prepare petition/complaint • Prepare & send demand (80% cases) • Maintain client communication • Serve the lawsuit	• Prepare & respond to discovery • Take & defend depositions • Prepare & argue motions • Prepare for mediation & trial • Maintain client communication	• Obtain release/order of dismissal • Resolve medical liens • Distribute funds to client and counsel • Request Google review • Close case file	• File & manage appeal • Maintain client communication • Achieve successful appellate resolution

This example shows how our firm defines each stage of the Client Journey, using clear Trigger Points and Objectives that must be met before moving to the next one. While your stages and Objectives will reflect your own practice, this model gives a sense of how it all comes together.

Before you start mapping, give some thought to whether you're mapping out one or multiple Pipelines. Ask yourself:

> Do our different case types follow the same basic journey, but with different tasks along the way? Personal injury cases—car accidents, slip-and-falls, dog bites—all follow the same stages, even though the specific work differs. If this describes your practice, one Pipeline works.
>
> Or do they require completely different paths from start to finish? If you do both criminal defense and estate planning, you'll likely require completely different workflows and timelines for each. If so, you need separate Pipelines.

If you need multiple Pipelines, work through the exercise for your highest-volume or highest-priority practice area first. Build others later, using the same process.

As you work through Steps 1–7 to organize your work, use the Pipeline Capture Sheet at the end of the exercise or at theset-up.co/workbookresources.

Step 1: Map the Boundaries

On your Pipeline Capture Sheet, write the start and end points of your typical case. Be specific about the triggering event that officially starts a case and the final action that closes it. For example:

> *Cases Begin When:* signed representation agreement is received and retainer is paid.
>
> *Cases End When:* final settlement is disbursed and file is archived.

Your boundary points should be concrete events anyone on your team can identify, not vague milestones, like "when we take the case" or "when it's done."

Step 2: Brain Dump Your Objectives

On paper, a whiteboard, or in a digital doc—whatever works for your brain—write down everything that happens in your typical case from start to finish; that's what we'll call the Client Journey. Think about every task, interaction, and decision point that happens along that journey. Also think about those wish-list items you want to make sure happen every time. These are your Objectives. You can't be too detailed at this point. Give yourself thirty to forty-five minutes to try to get everything out of your head—but don't worry if stuff lingers. You can always add more later.

Consider everything that happens from first contact to file closing:

- **Initial Contact and Intake:** how they find you, conflict checks, fee agreements, onboarding, prospect-to-client movement
- **Early Case Development:** initial filings, information gathering, client communications, expectation setting
- **Main Casework:** discovery, depositions, negotiations, motion practice, trial prep, court appearances
- **Resolution and Closing:** settlement documentation, final accounting, file closing, follow-up
- **Administrative/Back Office:** calendaring, billing, status updates, internal reviews, those tasks that often get forgotten
- **Client Touchpoints:** communications you want to happen consistently throughout the case

Step 3: Focus on Client Expectations

Your clients feel every gap in your process—the missed updates, the delays, the confusion about what's happening next. This step makes sure your Pipeline takes care of clients themselves, not just their cases.

Think like your client for a minute. What do they want from you? Regular updates so they're not wondering what's happening? Quick responses when they call? Understanding of what comes next? Write down three to five things that would make your typical client feel genuinely taken care of throughout their case.

If you need ideas, here are some client-focused Objectives that make a real difference.

- Send status update every two weeks (no news is still news).
- Call client before any major filing or court date.
- Provide "what happens next" explanation at each stage.
- Respond to calls/emails within four hours during business days.
- Send case closure summary with next steps (if any).

Add your client-focused Objectives to your brain dump from Step 2.

Step 4: Create Your First Pipeline Draft

Look at the list of Objectives you created in Steps 2 and 3 and start organizing them into stages on your Pipeline Capture Sheet. Stages, such as Intake, case building, discovery, and settlement negotiations, are formed by grouping Objectives that typically happen together. Ask yourself: Which tasks typically happen at the same time? What work needs to be completed before the next phase can begin? Where do cases naturally shift gears?

Keep it simple. Aim for no more than five stages, plus Intake. Name each stage based on what gets accomplished. Here's an example:

- **Intake:** Evaluate and Accept New Clients
- **Stage One:** Build Foundation (or Initiate Case)
- **Stage Two:** Discovery and Investigation (or Develop Case)
- **Stage Three:** Negotiate Resolution (or Prepare for Trial)
- **Stage Four:** Finalize and Close

Step 5: Refine Your Objectives

As you write them into each stage, keep in mind that Objectives need to be something someone can clearly check off as "done." Compare "handle discovery" (too vague) with "serve form interrogatories" or "review opposing party's discovery responses" (specific and clear). Test each Objective: Can someone know exactly when it's complete?

Also look for ways to group similar tasks into a single, streamlined Objective. For example:

> Instead of "order police reports," "order bodycam footage," and "request prosecutor's discovery," you could write: "Order all discovery materials from DA."
>
> Instead of separate entries for "retainer," "conflict check," and "intake form," use "complete intake packet."

Note: Your Pipeline tracks progress milestones. It answers the question "Where are we on this case?" It is *not* the place for the detailed how-to instructions. (Those live in your Process docs; we'll build those later.)

Once you're happy with your stages and Objectives, transfer them onto the Pipeline Capture Sheet under appropriate stage headings.

Step 6: Assign Roles

On your Pipeline Capture Sheet, decide who should handle each Objective—the Roles. And don't just go by job titles or specific team members' names; instead, think about what skills each task requires. That "lawyer work" you've been doing? Half of it probably doesn't need a lawyer.

For each Objective, ask: Does this require legal expertise, or could someone else handle it with proper training?

Here's a quick Role guide:

- **Attorney:** Legal analysis, strategy, court appearances
- **Paralegal/Legal Assistant:** Document prep, client communication, scheduling
- **Administrative Staff:** Data entry, filing, basic client contact
- **Case Manager:** Deadline tracking, team coordination, oversight

By assigning Roles by function rather than individuals' names, you make your Pipeline more flexible. When someone is out or leaves the firm, you know exactly what Objectives you need to cover and what type of Role can handle them.

Even if you're the one doing everything now, assigning Roles helps you prepare for delegation later. Map it the way your future team will work—even if today that's a "team of one."

Step 7: Define Trigger Points

You need clear signals that tell your team exactly when a case should move to the next stage. These are your Trigger Points—one concrete event (usually the last Objective in a stage) that anyone can recognize. Here are some examples.

- Intake → Stage One: Representation agreement signed
- Stage Two → Stage Three: Discovery complete
- Stage Four → Case Conclusion: Settlement reached or judgment entered

Add your Trigger Points to the Pipeline Capture Sheet. Also identify who updates case status when a Trigger Point is reached.

Document Your Pipeline

Your completed Pipeline Capture Sheet is your master plan—the blueprint everyone will follow. Save it in a shared location, where your whole team can access it and refer to it regularly. We'll talk about how to implement it in the next exercise.

Pipeline Capture Sheet

Instructions: Fill this out as you complete Steps 1-7 of Pipeline Exercise 1. This becomes your team's master reference document.

Pipeline Overview

Cases begin when: ______________________________

Cases end when: ______________________________

Total number of stages (not including Intake): ______________________________

Intake Stage

Stage Name: ______________________________

Objectives & Roles:

☐ ______________________ | Role: ______________________

☐ ______________________ | Role: ______________________

☐ ______________________ | Role: ______________________

☐ ______________________ | Role: ______________________

☐ ______________________ | Role: ______________________

Trigger to move to next Stage: ______________________________

Stage One

Stage Name: ______________________________

Objectives & Roles:

☐ ______________________ | Role: ______________________

☐ ______________________ | Role: ______________________

☐ ______________________ | Role: ______________________

☐ ______________________ | Role: ______________________

☐ ______________________ | Role: ______________________

Trigger to move to next Stage: ______________________

Stage Two

Stage Name: ______________________

Objectives & Roles:

☐ ______________________ | Role: ______________________

☐ ______________________ | Role: ______________________

☐ ______________________ | Role: ______________________

☐ ______________________ | Role: ______________________

☐ ______________________ | Role: ______________________

Trigger to move to next Stage: ______________________

Stage Three

Stage Name: ______________________

Objectives & Roles:

☐ ______________________ | Role: ______________________

☐ ______________________ | Role: ______________________

☐ ______________________ | Role: ______________________

☐ ______________________ | Role: ______________________

☐ ______________________ | Role: ______________________

Trigger to move to next Stage: ______________________________

Stage Four

Stage Name: ______________________________

Objectives & Roles:

- ☐ ______________________ | Role: ______________________
- ☐ ______________________ | Role: ______________________
- ☐ ______________________ | Role: ______________________
- ☐ ______________________ | Role: ______________________
- ☐ ______________________ | Role: ______________________

Trigger to move to next Stage: ______________________________

Stage Five (if needed)

Stage Name: ______________________________

Objectives & Roles:

- ☐ ______________________ | Role: ______________________
- ☐ ______________________ | Role: ______________________
- ☐ ______________________ | Role: ______________________
- ☐ ______________________ | Role: ______________________
- ☐ ______________________ | Role: ______________________

Trigger to move to next Stage: ______________________________

Pipeline Management

Who updates case status when each Trigger Point is reached?

Where is this Pipeline document stored/shared with the team?

Date of next Pipeline review: ______

Note: You can adapt this sheet based on your firm's needs. If you need fewer than five stages, leave sections blank. If you need more Objectives per stage, add them on the page or use separate sheets of paper.

Pipeline Exercise 2. Implement Your Pipeline

Now that you've built your Pipeline, it's time to put it into action. The key is to start small and grow from there.

Step 1: Soft Launch

Test your Pipeline with two or three new cases. Don't try to retrofit existing cases for the new system. That's a recipe for frustration and confusion. Let legacy cases stay in their current workflow while you prove the new system works on fresh matters.

During this phase, work closely with the core team members who helped build the Pipeline. They understand the logic behind the stages and Objectives, which makes them your best allies for spotting what works and what needs adjustment. Their buy-in also helps when you roll it out to the broader team.

Keep the soft launch period appropriate for your practice area. If you handle criminal defense or family law matters that move quickly, a few weeks might be enough. If you're in personal injury or complex litigation, you may need a couple of months to see cases progress through multiple stages.

After your soft launch period ends, gather your core team for a debrief. Ask: What worked? What felt clunky? Did any Objectives need rewording? Were Trigger Points clear? Did anyone get stuck wondering whose job something was? This is your chance to catch friction points before rolling the Pipeline out to everyone.

Adjust the Pipeline Capture Sheet based on what you learned. Update stage names if they were confusing. Revise Objectives that were too vague or too granular. Clarify Roles where there was ambiguity. Add any missing client touchpoints you discovered. Don't skip this step—training your team on a system that still has obvious problems will undermine confidence in the whole thing.

Once you've refined the Pipeline based on real use, you're ready to train the full team.

Step 2: Team Training

Bring your team together and show them the Pipeline by giving them a copy of your Pipeline document or conducting the whiteboard exercise I discuss in chapter 4 of *The Set-Up*.

You can use this script as a guide.

Thanks for being here, everyone. I want to show you something that will make all of our lives easier. This is our new Pipeline. It's a map of how a case moves through our firm, from first contact to resolution. Instead of guessing what's next or waiting on me, the Pipeline lays the progression out clearly.

Each stage marks a checkpoint. Inside are Objectives—the tasks that move the case forward—with Roles assigned so it's always clear who's responsible. At the end of each stage come the Trigger Points. These are the signals that move a case from one stage to the next. When you hit a Trigger Point, you also update the Pipeline dashboard, so we always know where a case stands.

Why are we doing this? Because we've all felt the frustration of things slipping through the cracks or repeating instructions. The Pipeline takes that weight off me as the bottleneck and off you as the ones left guessing.

[Close by inviting input.]

What questions do you have? What looks helpful? What feels like it might not work in your day-to-day? The more feedback you share now, the stronger this system will be for all of us.

After training, apply the Pipeline to each new case as it comes in. Then, as cases move through the Pipeline, stay alert and watch out for confusion or stalls. If multiple people ask the same question or cases consistently slow at the same point, that's your signal to adjust. Quick check-ins with your team will surface issues early: What's unclear? Where are you getting stuck? Small refinements now prevent bigger problems later.

Be sure to add your Pipeline rollout to your Set-Up Quarterly Plan. Include soft launch date, team training date, and a thirty-day check-in to review what's working.

Pipeline Exercise 3. Set Up a Dashboard

The Pipeline lays out the Client Journey, with what needs to happen and who's responsible for doing it. And honestly, just having that structure in place will bring more calm than you've probably felt in years.

But a Pipeline on its own is like a beautifully drawn map folded up in your desk. It shows you the route, but it doesn't tell you how the trip is going. That's why you need a Pipeline dashboard. The dashboard is your live readout. It tells you not only what *should happen* but what *is happening*. It shows you which cases are on track, which ones are stalled, and where the next action sits.

Your dashboard doesn't have to be a spreadsheet full of columns and headers. Or a huge readout from your case management system (CMS). To manage your Pipeline and track your case flow, the dashboard can be quite simple, with just a few important columns:

- **Case/Matter:** a short identifier like the client's name, matter number, or case description.
- **Current Stage:** the stage of the Pipeline the case is in right now (Intake, Stage One, Stage Two, etc.). This gives you a snapshot of your entire caseload at a glance. Instead of guessing or digging through files, you can see exactly where each case sits in the journey and whether it's moving forward or stuck.
- **Stage Entry Date:** the date the case moved into its current stage. This tells you how long cases are sitting in one spot. If a case has lingered longer than usual, that's a signal: There's either a bottleneck to fix or a risk of delay that could affect your client's outcome and your revenue flow.
- **Anticipated Value:** your best estimate of what the case is worth. You're not locking it in—just setting a reserve, like an insurance company would—so it doesn't have to be exact to the penny. Tracking Anticipated Value across your dashboard lets you see your revenue in motion and spot the impact of stalled cases on your bottom line.
- **Anticipated Settlement Date:** your best estimate of when the case will wrap up. Again, this doesn't have to be perfect. The goal is to see how your caseload lines up with your cash flow. If several cases stall, you'll see revenue gaps appear on the dashboard. That gives you a clear early warning, whether you need to address a bottleneck in your Pipeline or push harder on marketing to bring in fresh cases.

These five fields are enough to give you a clear picture of your caseload and revenue in motion. Here's what it looks like in practice.

Case/Matter	Current Stage	Stage Entry Date	Anticipated Value	Anticipated Settlement Date
Smith v. ABC Corp	Stage Two	03/15/2024	$45,000	09/15/2024
Jones Car Accident	Intake	03/20/2024	$25,000	12/20/2024
Wilson Slip & Fall	Stage Three	02/28/2024	$75,000	06/30/2024

Your dashboard should be accessible to everyone involved in case management. Whether you use a shared spreadsheet, your CMS, or another platform, make sure your team can view it in real time. Transparency keeps everyone aligned, reduces the "what's happening with this case?" questions, and reinforces that the Pipeline is a team system, not just the leader's tracking tool.

Making the Dashboard Work

Now let's talk about how to actually use this tool. The dashboard earns its keep only when it becomes part of your rhythm. Reviewing the Pipeline dashboard in your weekly Set-Up Time or perhaps in a short weekly review with your team keeps cases moving, spots stalled files before they become crises, and helps you plan around revenue gaps.

Look for patterns like these:

- **Bottlenecks:** If several cases linger at the same stage for weeks, that's a signal. For example, if three cases are stuck at Stage Two and all are waiting on medical records, the problem isn't slow cases; it's the records process that needs fixing.
- **Revenue Gaps:** If Stage Three is packed with high-value cases set to resolve soon but the next quarter looks empty, you've got a cash flow issue in the making. You either need to move earlier-stage cases faster or make money management decisions so you can weather the lull.

- **Client Delays:** If clients complain that nothing's happening and your dashboard shows their cases have been stalled twice as long as usual in Stage One, that's a system breakdown you can fix before it spreads.
- **Handoffs:** If cases consistently slow down when moving from Stage One (handled by your paralegal) to Stage Two (handled by you), that's often a handoff problem disguised as workload. Your dashboard will show the pattern so you can fix it before things in your Pipeline begin to back up.

The integrity of the system depends on consistency. Whoever completes a Trigger Point must update the dashboard immediately—especially the Current Stage and Stage Entry Date columns. Additionally, review and update your Anticipated Value and Anticipated Settlement Date columns regularly to reflect changes in case dynamics or new information. Without those steps, decisions get made on guesses instead of facts. When updates happen in real time, the dashboard becomes a living management tool you can trust.

Finally, the platform itself matters less than the discipline. Consistency is what transforms the dashboard from a chart on paper into your firm's command center: an early-warning system, a planning tool, and proof that nothing is slipping through the cracks.

Add your dashboard set-up and rhythm review to your Set-Up Quarterly Plan.

people
your core

THE PEOPLE PILLAR is where everything real lives.

It's about the actual humans in your firm. It's about their trust, their voices, their fears, and their fire. It's about how you show up as a leader when things are messy and how your team shows up for each other when no one's watching. The People pillar is the core, the heart of your firm. Harder to measure, yes, but impossible to fake.

In this chapter, you'll look at what's really going on. You'll reflect on your leadership. The honest version, not just the polished one. You'll name a mission and values that live not just in a handbook, but in conversations, decisions, and everyday moments. You'll take the pulse of your firm's climate. Not just the version you'd pitch in an interview, but the one that shows up in text threads, inside jokes, and how people feel after a hard day.

This part is vulnerable because it asks you to tell the truth. But it also builds the People pillar piece by piece: strong leadership, real purpose, shared values, and a culture where people can breathe.

Need a Refresher?

Go back to *The Set-Up*:

Chapter 5: It All Depends on You, if you need a reminder that your firm really is a mirror of your leadership (even on the days you'd rather not look).

Chapter 6: What Kind of Leader Are You, Really?, when you want the full tour through the six archetypes. It's long, so maybe grab a snack first.

Chapter 7: The Practice of Phenomenal Leadership, when you're ready for the "okay, now what?" part and the core practices that pull it all together.

Chapter 8: What Is Your "Why"?, if you need a reminder of why your mission and values are the bedrock of culture (and how easy it is to slide into the dreaded default culture if you're not intentional).

Chapter 9: Putting Your Why Into Action, if you need a reminder of how values take root only when they're embedded into your team's day-to-day.

People Exercise 1. Leadership Self-Assessment

If I could blame the market for why firms struggle, I would. Or the competition down the street. Or the belief there are no good people to hire. It'd sure be easier. But the truth is the biggest factor in whether your firm stands or sinks comes down to one thing: you, its leader.

Look closely, and you'll see it, too. The motion that never made it to the judge's desk. The client who lost confidence after weeks without an update. The paralegal who finally walked when the workload never let up. On the surface, they look like separate problems. But they're not. They all trace back to the same place: leadership. Did we set the pace? Did we create systems that made follow-through nonnegotiable? Did we build clarity for the team and show consistency ourselves?

Exhausting, I know. But there's grace here, too. Because leadership isn't fixed, and it's not some genetic lottery ticket you either won or didn't. It's a practice. Which means, with some self-awareness, some courage, and a willingness to look in the mirror, you can change. You can raise the ceiling on what your firm is capable of. What does that look like? It looks like what I call being a Phenomenal Leader, *the kind of leader whose team wants the firm's success as much as they do.*

That's the vision behind the leadership self-assessment. It pulls from the strengths of leadership archetypes—the practices of Phenomenal Leadership—and hands you a mirror. So, before you start, promise yourself honesty. The kind that stings a little. And if that's too hard, ask someone you trust to walk through it with you. Growth in leadership rarely comes with fireworks. It comes with showing up. Again, and then again.

Step 1: Do the Assessment

Read through the questions under each quality. For each one, rate how well and how consistently you demonstrate that behavior. Give yourself an honest rating next to each item.

Rating Scale

E = Exceptional: You consistently demonstrate this at a high level.

S = Satisfactory: You demonstrate this regularly and adequately.

NI = Needs Improvement: You demonstrate this inconsistently or need to strengthen it.

U = Unsatisfactory: You rarely or never demonstrate this.

Empowers Through Service and Support

The best leaders aren't the heroes of the story; they're the ones clearing the path so others can run. That means removing obstacles, sharing credit, and building leaders who will one day lead without you.

____ Do I actively remove obstacles that prevent my team from doing their best work?

____ Am I developing future leaders within the firm?

____ Do team members feel empowered to contribute meaningfully?

____ Are there structures for team accountability and ownership?

____ Do I give my team the tools and resources they need to succeed?

Stays Engaged Without Micromanaging

Nobody thrives under a microscope. And nobody thrives when their leader vanishes either. The real art is in staying close enough to support and guide but far enough to let people own their work. That balance is what builds trust and keeps you from burning out, too.

____ Do I provide guidance without hovering?

____ Am I clear in my expectations while allowing autonomy?

____ Do I offer timely, constructive feedback?

____ Are people encouraged to take initiative and bring new ideas forward?

____ Does our firm support flexible, adaptive work where possible?

Balances Confidence with Humility

No one wants a leader who wavers on every decision or one who barrels through without listening. The art is somewhere in the middle: bold enough to decide, humble enough to change course when needed. This balance is what keeps your team steady and willing to follow you.

____ Do I make decisions decisively, without second-guessing?

____ Am I open to feedback and willing to change my mind?

____ Do I create a safe environment for input and ideas?

____ Do I lead by example in living out the firm's values?

____ Do team members know how their work supports our mission?

Cultivates a Growth Mindset

A stagnant team is a dying team. The best leaders model curiosity, resilience, and the willingness to learn even when it's uncomfortable. If you're still growing, your team has permission to grow, too. If you're not, you've quietly told them to stop.

____ Do I encourage learning and development in the team?

____ Am I committed to my own growth?

____ Is feedback welcomed and seen as a tool for growth?

____ Are mistakes treated as learning opportunities?

____ Do we create time for team building and reflection?

Guides with Vision and Purpose

It's not enough to work hard. People want to know where they're headed and why it matters. Vision gives direction; purpose gives meaning. Without them, even the most talented team will drift, working hard but going nowhere.

____ Do I communicate a clear, compelling vision?

____ Can I adapt plans without losing alignment?

____ Does my team understand how their work connects to the firm's goals?

____ Do I regularly share updates on firm's progress?

____ Is there a strong sense of shared purpose?

Leads with Emotional Intelligence

Skills and strategy will get you only so far. What your team remembers is how you handle conflict, stress, and mistakes. Do you lose your cool or listen? Do you shut people down or draw them out? Emotional intelligence is what builds trust or breaks it.

____ Am I aware of how my emotions affect my leadership?

____ Do I handle conflict with empathy?

____ Do I manage my own stress and help others do the same?

____ Do I handle underperformance while maintaining trust?

____ Do I visibly recognize commitment and contribution?

HOW DO you feel after going through that list? Do you see places where you're strong? Areas that need attention? Use the steps ahead to reflect, choose areas of focus, and commit to improving your leadership.

Step 2: See What's Strong

Go back through your answers. Count how many E's and S's you gave yourself and write the numbers below. These are your strengths. Then, list a few of your highest-rated behaviors below. Celebrate them. This is the infrastructure your People pillar is built on.

E: ________

S: ________

List two–three specific behaviors you rated as E or S:

Step 3: Name What Needs Attention

Look across the six leadership qualities. Which areas have the most NI and U ratings? These represent your biggest opportunities for growth.

List your areas for growth (NI/U ratings):

Step 4: Choose and Commit

From the areas you listed in Step 3, pick one or two to focus on first. If you're not sure, choose the ones causing the most immediate strain in your firm right now. Turn your choices into SMART goals and put them on your calendar to work on during your Set-Up Time. For example:

"By [date], I will schedule biweekly one-on-one check-ins with each team member to improve communication and connection."

"Starting on [date], I will ask for feedback at the end of every team meeting to gauge clarity and team alignment."

Goals to improve leadership:

1 __________

2 __________

Step 5: Get Feedback, Build Accountability

Ask your team how they experience your leadership. You can even give them a copy of the assessment and ask them to rate you. Yes, this takes courage. But leaders who ask are the ones who grow. Write down one concrete way you'll ask (e.g., survey, one-on-ones, anonymous feedback).

How will you get their input?

Step 6: Keep Growing

Pick one tool or resource that will stretch you: a leadership podcast on your commute, a peer group you join monthly, a book you work through chapter by chapter during your Set-Up Time. The point isn't which one you choose, it's that you choose something and use it. Write it down. Put it on your calendar.

I will:

Step 7: Schedule Your Next Check-In

Growth isn't one and done. Pick a date six months from now to retake this assessment. Write it in your calendar *today*.

Date of next check-in: ______________________

Carry your goals into your Set-Up Quarterly Plan so they become part of your firm's growth strategy.

People Exercise 2. What's Our Why? Workshop

Every firm is telling a story, whether you've written it down or not. The question is, Is it a story your people believe in?

Your mission is the heartbeat of that story. It's why you keep going when the case feels impossible and the hours blur together. When you're staring at another stack of depositions at midnight, your mission reminds you why the work matters.

Your values, on the other hand, are how you live out your story. They're how you show up when opposing counsel plays dirty, how you handle the client who's falling apart, and how your team reacts when the workload feels crushing. Together, they're what makes your firm more than just a business. They make it a place of belonging and purpose. A place for fulfilling the reason you chose to practice law in the first place.

You and your team can do this workshop to name your firm's mission, define your core values, and embed your values into your day-to-day, which are foundational to creating a healthy firm culture.

Objective: To develop a mission statement and core values that resonate with your team, define your firm's identity, and align with its aspirations.

Time Needed: Two to three hours

Materials Needed:

- Whiteboard (or large flip chart) and markers for mission drafting
- Sticky notes (lots) and thick markers (easy to read from six to eight feet)
- A list of words to describe core values (you can find a list of examples at theset-up.co/workbookresources)
- A big wall or foam board for clustering notes
- Timer (to keep things moving and focused)
- Phone/camera (to capture the wall/board before you clean up)
- Mission and Core Values Capture Sheet on page 46 (or at theset-up.co/workbookresources)
- Snacks and water (trust me, it helps)
- Remote-friendly substitutions, like a Zoom/Teams whiteboard

Step 1: Gather the Right People

Invite anyone who shapes the client experience—lawyers, paralegals, Intake team, front desk, ops. Gather around a whiteboard or flip chart. (Remote teams can use your virtual whiteboard.)

Choose someone to facilitate the workshop so the conversation stays on track. This could be you, one of your partners, or even a trusted colleague from outside the firm, who can guide the process and let you participate fully alongside your team. The facilitator's role is to keep time, ask follow-up questions when the room gets quiet, and make sure everyone contributes.

Set the tone with words like the following:

> We're here to put into words what makes our firm strong—our purpose and the values we want to live by. These will guide how we work together and how clients experience us. Every voice in this room matters, because we each play a part in shaping our culture. So, speak up. Share what you believe and listen for the common threads that connect us.

Step 2: Draft a Mission Statement (30 to 45 minutes)

Your mission is your purpose—why your firm exists—in one or two sentences.

Explain the purpose of the exercise. For example:

> A mission is our purpose. The reason we exist as a firm. Think of it as our North Star. It answers three simple questions: Who do we serve? What do we do best? And why does it matter? Our mission should be short and clear, something anyone here could say out loud in a sentence or two. It guides our decisions, keeps us focused, and reminds us why the work we do matters. That's why we're creating it together today.

On the board, draw three columns, labeled: "Who do we serve?" "What do we deliver to our clients?" and "Why does it matter?"

Ask the group to call out short answers and record them in the appropriate columns. Don't overthink it. Just capture phrases and keywords. Use the examples below for inspiration, then create your own.

Who do we serve?	What do we deliver to our clients?	Why does it matter?
Injured people	Justice against powerful defendants	So clients can rebuild their lives
Families planning for the future	Clear, conflict-free estate plans	So loved ones have peace of mind
Parents in custody disputes	Guidance through family transitions with dignity	So children are protected and supported
People facing criminal charges	Strong defense of constitutional rights	So every person receives a fair defense

Take the strongest answers from the columns and arrange them into one of the below templates. These aren't meant to be rigid, just a starting point to get the words flowing.

Template 1: We [what] for [who] so they can [outcome/why].

Template 2: To [verb] [who] by [how/what] with [values/approach].

Write a few versions on the board so the group can compare them. Here are some examples for inspiration:

- We stand with the injured, fighting for the resources they need to rebuild their lives.
- We help families plan wisely so their legacy brings peace instead of conflict.
- To protect the rights of the accused and ensure every person receives a fair defense.

Once you've got a couple of drafts on the board, read each one aloud and ask: Is it clear in under ten seconds? Would a new hire "get it" on day one? Does it sound like us?

Tighten until there's agreement. Edit right there on the board—cross out words, swap phrases, simplify. Keep going until the group hears one version and everyone nods: "That's it." You'll know it in your gut.

Step 3: Identify Your Core Values (30 to 45 minutes)

Your values are your principles in action. In other words, *how* you show up day-to-day. You're going to aim for five to seven in total. Have the list of core values you downloaded handy to circulate for reference throughout this exercise.

The facilitator should kick this part of the workshop off with a few grounding words. For example:

> The purpose of this exercise is to name the values that define who we are as a firm. These are the real standards we will hold ourselves to every day. They should guide how we treat clients, how we work with each other, and how we make decisions. At the end of the exercise, we want to walk away with five to seven values that truly feel like us.

They might also add: "There are no wrong answers here. Every idea is welcome. Think about the moments you've been proud to be part of this firm or the times you've seen us at our best. That's what we're trying to capture."

Give each person a stack of sticky notes and a marker. Ask them to write one idea per sticky note on their own for five to seven minutes. Prompts you can say out loud to get the creative juices flowing:

- What sets our firm apart?
- What are we most proud of?
- How do we want clients to experience us?
- How do we want to treat each other on an ordinary Tuesday?
- What kind of impact do we want to have on clients, courts, community, and each other?

Have everyone come up and place their stickies on the wall or board, where the whole team can see all the ideas together.

As a group, move stickies with a common theme into clusters. For example, all the stickies about integrity, honesty, and doing the right thing might form one cluster. Then, once you've grouped similar ideas, label each cluster with a single value word or phrase that captures the theme. Keep it short and memorable (one to three words).

For each cluster, write one sentence to answer the question: What does this look like in our firm? The key here is to keep the language plain and real. Here are some examples.

Value word	What this looks like in our firm
Growth	We ask questions when we don't know, celebrate each other's wins, and see feedback as a gift, not an attack.
Integrity	We keep promises, act with transparency, and do the right thing, even when it's hard.
Justice	We take cases that matter, fight for the underdog, and won't compromise our principles for a bigger fee.
Resilience	We bounce back from bad days, support each other through tough cases, and find ways to laugh even when the work is heavy.

Now, step back and look at the wall together. Ask: Which values feel most central to who we are as a firm? Which themes show up repeatedly across different people's stickies?

Select five to seven values that most resonate and, finally, conduct a pressure test: Can we see this value in action not just today but next week and the weeks after? Would we hire/fire/promote by it? Could we explain it to a client in plain English?

Most firms quit after Step 3. Don't. Beautiful values on a wall never changed a single client's experience or a firm's day-to-day. They only work when they start showing up—in decisions, in processes, in daily habits. If you stop here, nothing changes.

Step 4 is where you prove your values mean something.

Step 4: Make It Real (30 to 40 minutes)

Turn to the Values in Action list that follows. As a team, scan through the 30 items and put a checkmark next to any that feel relevant to or interesting for your firm. The idea is to mark the ones that spark recognition or excitement.

From the items you mark, choose three or four that feel most doable in the next 30 to 60 days. (And listen, this list isn't meant to overwhelm you. You won't do all 30 next month. The goal is to pick a few high-impact actions, make them stick, then come back for more.) Ask yourselves: Which ones could we start this week? Which ones address our biggest gaps right now? Which ones would our clients notice?

Write your chosen items on the board and assign owners to head up each initiative.

Schedule a 90-day review where you'll assess how you're doing with these commitments and potentially add more items from the list. Put them in everyone's calendar now.

Step 5: Document Your Mission and Core Values

Before you wrap up, fill out your Mission and Core Values Capture Sheet. Save it in a shared location, where your team can access it, then record that location in your Set-Up Quarterly Plan to emphasize its importance in your firm's growth strategy. That way, today's work becomes part of how your firm runs.

Values in Action: 30 Practical Ways to Impact Your Firm's Culture

In Communication

- ☐ Reference values in meetings
- ☐ Celebrate value-based wins
- ☐ Use values in feedback
- ☐ Explain decisions through values
- ☐ Repeat values regularly

In Hiring & Onboarding

- ☐ Interview for values
- ☐ Ask behavioral questions
- ☐ Include values in job descriptions
- ☐ Teach values in onboarding
- ☐ Assign value-based mentors

In Policies & Operations

- ☐ Include values in performance reviews
- ☐ Tie discipline back to reflection of values
- ☐ Build a formal feedback process
- ☐ Weave values into Process
- ☐ Clean up outdated policies

In Decision-Making

- ☐ Use values to guide client selection
- ☐ Apply values to hard decisions
- ☐ Ask "What does this say about us?"
- ☐ Walk away from misaligned opportunities
- ☐ Publicly reward value-based decisions

In the Community

- ☐ Support causes aligned with your values
- ☐ Volunteer in value-aligned ways
- ☐ Spotlight your team's community work
- ☐ Partner with like-minded organizations
- ☐ Say no to misaligned sponsorships

In the Day-to-Day

- ☐ Start meetings with a values check-in
- ☐ Make space for team gratitude
- ☐ Use values to recover from mistakes
- ☐ Tell value-aligned stories
- ☐ Create a Wins & Values Wall

Mission and Core Values Capture Sheet

Use this space to record your results.

Final Mission Statement

Core Values

(five to seven values with behaviors)

1 Value:

What this looks like in our firm:

2 Value:

What this looks like in our firm:

3 Value: ____________________

What this looks like in our firm: ____________________

4 Value: ____________________

What this looks like in our firm: ____________________

5 Value: ____________________

What this looks like in our firm: ____________________

6 Value: ____________________

What this looks like in our firm: ____________________

7 Value: ____________________

What this looks like in our firm: ____________________

Next Steps: Making It Real

First three or four actions we commit to in the next 30–60 days:

1 ____________________ (Owner: ____________________)

2 ____________________ (Owner: ____________________)

3 ____________________ (Owner: ____________________)

4 ____________________ (Owner: ____________________)

90-Day Check-In Date: ____________________

Where this document is stored/shared: ____________________

____

People Exercise 3. Firm's Climate Action Plan

The climate of your firm is the weather your people breathe every day. Some days it's bright and clear. You can feel the energy, the possibility humming in the air. Other days it feels like a storm rolling in, heavy and unpredictable, and everyone's walking on eggshells.

At the heart of that weather is psychological safety—whether your people can exhale fully, speak their truth, mess up without shame, and offer their wildest ideas without bracing for impact. Without psychological safety, your mission statement might as well be wallpaper. Your carefully crafted values can't take root in soil that's too hard, too scared, or too guarded. The truth is people can't bring their best selves to work if they don't feel safe doing it.

Climate, though, isn't the same as culture. Culture is what you intentionally build from your mission and values—or what accidentally forms when you don't. Climate is how that culture shows up day-to-day, in every interaction, decision, and response. When you shape climate with intention, culture thrives. When you ignore the daily weather, it hardens into what I call a default culture—that toxic, firm-crushing pattern that takes over when no one's steering.

But a healthy climate doesn't just happen. It's shaped by the leader (or leaders) with every interaction, every response to conflict, and every time you choose curiosity over judgment—or don't. In short, the weather in your firm starts with you.

Use this during your Set-Up Time to take an honest look at the climate you're shaping. Then make it a monthly check-in. Five minutes to read the room and ask yourself: What's the weather been like around here lately? What small adjustment could steady the climate this week? We are working with humans after all—messy, wonderful, and fascinating as they are—so pay attention to the weather changes.

Firm's Climate Quick Check

Read through each of the six climate factors below and jot down what you notice. (These are discussed at length in Daniel Goleman's article "Leadership That Gets Results," pp. 79–90.) Be honest. These are the signals of your climate and the daily proof of how it feels to work at your firm.

Elements of a Healthy Climate

Flexibility: Can team members get things done without red tape or being second-guessed?

Responsibility: How much ownership do people feel toward the firm and its clients?

Performance Standards: Are expectations clear and consistent, or do they shift?

Feedback and Rewards: Is feedback fair and specific or vague and inconsistent?

Clarity: Does everyone understand the mission, values, and direction?

Commitment: Are people pulling together with a sense of shared purpose?

Climate Reflection Prompts

Which factor feels strongest right now?

Which one feels most fragile?

Do people feel safe to speak up, admit mistakes, and offer new ideas here?

What's one small action you could take this month to steady the climate?

Steadying Your Firm's Climate: Quick Wins for Leaders

Pick one or two of these to try this week. Once you feel good about how that works, pick another one.

- ☐ **Go first:** In your next team meeting, admit one thing you could've handled better. Watch how it opens the door for honesty.
- ☐ **Say thank you:** When someone brings up a concern, start with "Thanks for raising that." It lowers the temperature right away.
- ☐ **Close the loop:** If someone shares an idea, circle back—even if just to say "I didn't forget; here's where it stands." That builds trust.
- ☐ **Check the room:** Ask "Did I miss anything important?" or invite someone quiet to share what they see.
- ☐ **Celebrate small wins:** End the week by pointing out one quiet win—or leave a quick note on someone's desk that says, "I noticed what you did—thank you."
- ☐ **Protect against blame:** Instead of "Who messed this up?" ask "What in our system broke down here?"

Your Firm's Climate Action Plan

Based on your reflection above, what's the one factor that needs attention first?

Who will you ask to help you notice if the climate is improving?

What specific action will you take this month?

Record it in your Set-Up Quarterly Plan.

process
your engine

YOUR PIPELINE tells you *what* needs to happen and *who* does it. It maps the checkpoints a case must hit and who's responsible for each. Process is the *how*. That's where you spell out the step-by-step mechanics of the Pipeline Objectives. Take this family law example:

Pipeline: "Serve discovery and calendar deadlines."

Process: "Draft interrogatories, finalize RFPs, track the thirty-day due date, enter deadlines in the system."

See the difference? The Pipeline keeps the flow clear and visible for everyone. The Process brings those Objectives to life with detailed instructions. Without documented Processes, you're still a walking instruction manual. People come to you for routine guidance, handle tasks inconsistently, and can't cover for each other when someone's out. New hires spend weeks learning "how we do things" through trial and error because the knowledge lives in people's heads, not in writing.

Process is also what makes non-case stuff—onboarding, time off, client communications—work consistently. Without it, you're always one sick day or departing employee away from chaos.

That said, overprocessing creates its own chaos. When you try to systematize everything, you end up with process paralysis, where people spend more time checking procedures than doing work. Your team becomes robotic instead of thoughtful, following scripts for conversations that should be natural and consulting flowcharts for decisions that require judgment. Focus on the work that happens regularly, the stuff that causes confusion, or the tasks that directly touch your clients' lives. Let the rest be what it is.

This section walks you through creating your firm's Process: documenting what works, filling the gaps, and building systems that ensure your people follow your directions. The goal is simple: Your firm should run predictably, whether you're there or not.

Need a Refresher?

Go back to *The Set-Up*:

Chapter 10: The Invisible Engine, if you need a reminder that Process is what keeps the work moving. Without it, things stall. With it, your team knows what to do next.

Process Exercise 1. Record and Align What You're Already Doing

The first step in creating your firm's Process is simple: Write down the processes you're already using and align them with your Pipeline Objectives. For the Objectives where nothing's documented yet—or where "the process" is just whatever happens—you'll create the processes from scratch in Exercise 2.

Building your Process will take time. But just like with the other foundational aspects of your firm, the time you invest now will pay off significantly. You can sit down in one long session and get the processes for your most important Objectives (the ones that happen most frequently or cause the most confusion) hammered out.

If that's not a luxury you can afford, create processes for just one or two Objectives now, then come back next week and choose one or two more. Even if you start with one or two new processes, you'll feel the impact immediately, and it might be just the boost you need to keep going. The beauty is that once your Process is in place, you won't need to revisit it in such depth again.

As you work through the steps below, use the Process Capture Sheet at the end of this chapter or at theset-up.co/workbookresources to document each process. You'll complete one sheet per Objective. These will become your Process library—the reference your team will use to maintain consistency.

Step 1: Pick Your Battle

Choose an Objective in your Pipeline that's driving you crazy. Look for one that

- happens regularly
- requires precision
- varies depending on who does it
- causes confusion or slows things down
- directly impacts the client experience

Common culprits are Objectives such as client intake calls that miss key information, medical record requests that sit in limbo, and discovery responses that require three rounds of "did you remember to..."

Write your chosen Objective at the top of your Process Capture Sheet.

Step 2: Gather Your Team

Your team already knows what's working and what's not. Don't document this process alone. Bring in whoever in your office does this work. You'll be more accurate, catch real decision points, and get buy-in from day one.

On your Process Capture Sheet, note who usually handles this Objective.

Step 3: Capture Reality

Forget perfect. Just brain dump what really happens today and those things that should happen but often get overlooked. List the steps in order under Step-by-Step on your Process Capture Sheet. Be specific enough that someone unfamiliar with the task could follow along.

Step 4: Map the If/Then

Here's where most firms mess up. They document the happy path—what happens when everything goes perfectly. But real processes need to handle the curveballs. In *The Set-Up*, I explain it in terms of algorithmic thinking: "If X, then Y." So here, you are spelling out what you do when processes don't follow ideal scenarios.

For example, what happens when

- the client doesn't respond? If there is no response after three days, then send follow-up text and email.
- documents are missing? If you are missing records, then call hospital records department directly and escalate to supervisor.
- the deadline passes? If a deadline is missed, then notify attorney immediately and send expedited request with a rush fee.
- the hospital requires a different authorization form? If you have the wrong form, then use their template and have client re-sign within 24 hours.

In the Decision Points (If/Then) section of your Process Capture Sheet, document the curveballs and responses for your process. Keep adding branches each time you refine the process.

Step 5: Bundle and Streamline

Now that you've documented the complete process with decision points, you're ready to think bigger. You can save your team serious time by bundling related Objectives under one process. For example, instead of creating four separate processes for requesting, reviewing, summarizing, and sending medical records, create one Medical Records to Damages process:

- Legal assistant requests records within five days of signing.
- Legal assistant reviews within 48 hours of receipt.
- Legal assistant calculates damages estimate.
- Lawyer prepares demand based on the completed summary.

Result: Four separate processes become one streamlined workflow. The legal assistant handles all records work in sequence without interruption; the lawyer receives complete and organized information ready for the demand, and nothing gets lost in handoffs.

Take a high-level look at your Pipeline and use the Opportunities to Streamline section on your Process Capture Sheet to note:

- What Objectives naturally flow together?
- What information are people handling multiple times?
- Where could you bundle client communications?
- What processes involve the same deadlines?

Choose one bundle of Objectives and, using Steps 2 to 4 above, create a single process for it on a new Process Capture Sheet.

Step 6: Write It Down

Processes don't help if no one can find them. Store your completed Process Capture Sheets where your team will look, such as in a shared folder, a Google Doc, or OneNote. Make them something easy to access and update. Also be sure to use clear names that make sense to tired brains at 4:00 p.m.: "Process—Client Intake."

We store our Process Capture Sheets here:

____

____

____

Step 7: Train and Refine

Creating a Process is only half the battle. Getting your team to use it is where most firms stumble.

Assign a team member as the go-to for Process. Then, follow the same implementation steps you used for your Pipeline—team meeting, process owner, two-week check-in. Don't just email your team a document and hope for the best. Most processes need at least one round of refinement based on how they work in practice. This isn't failure; it's feedback. Make any tweaks, communicate changes to everyone immediately, and build the final version into your onboarding routine for new hires.

Document the Process owner and your two-week check-in date on your Process Capture Sheet. *Add these to your Set-Up Quarterly Plan.*

Process Exercise 2. Creating New Processes (When None Exist)

Some Objectives you mapped in your Pipeline won't have existing processes, probably because you have added new Objectives to your Pipeline, or there isn't one consistent way things are being done. This means you have an opportunity to create a new process.

One quick way to get started is to use AI as a drafting partner. Give it a clear, specific prompt, and you'll have a rough framework in seconds. Then, use the same steps you've already practiced in Process Exercise 1 to make it work for your firm. Here are some prompts you can try when you hit a blank page.

- Create a five-step process for gathering medical records from hospitals, including a follow-up when records are incomplete.
- Generate a process for scheduling depositions that covers coordinating with opposing counsel and preparing clients.
- Create a simple process for sending meeting reminders.
- Generate a workflow for logging phone calls with clients.
- Develop a checklist for organizing digital client files.
- Build a process for internal deadline tracking.
- Create a follow-up system after consultations.

Remember: AI doesn't know your tools, your deadlines, or your team, so it can't give you the final version. But it can break the blank-page barrier so you and your team can finish it together.

Your Objective that needs a process:

____

____

Your AI prompt:

____

____

Document your new process on your Process Capture Sheet. *Record any implementation goals in your Set-Up Quarterly Plan.*

Process Exercise 3. Firm Operations Processes

Not every process is tied to your Pipeline. Some of the messiest, most time-consuming work happens in the spaces between cases—hiring, onboarding, time-off requests, billing. These firm operations need processes, too.

Step 1: Identify Your Friction Points

Walk through a typical week and note where you think: "This always takes longer than it should" or "Why do we keep having to figure this out?" Common areas that need processes:

- Onboarding new hires (from offer letter to day one)
- Team time-off requests (how they're submitted, tracked, approved)
- Billing and invoicing (time tracking, sending invoices, following up)
- Training and development (CLEs, mentoring, internal training)
- Client communication (who sends what, when, and how)
- File management (naming, storing, and accessing client files)
- Equipment and technology (ordering, set-up, troubleshooting)

Pick one area that causes the most confusion or eats up the most time each week. Start here—you can tackle others later, using the same approach.

Step 2: Document the Process

Grab a new Process Capture Sheet. Write the name of your firm operations process (e.g., "New hire onboarding" or "Time-off request process") in the allotted spot. Then follow the same documentation steps as in Process Exercise 1.

Process Capture Sheet

Pipeline Objective/Firm Operations Process: ______________________

Who usually handles it? ______________________

Step-by-Step

(what happens today)

Who kicks off the process?

____

____

____

____

What's Step 1?

____

____

____

____

Then what?

____

____

____

____

Tools or software used

Templates, forms, or scripts involved

How do you know when it's done?

How is completion tracked?

Decision Points (If/Then)

If ______________________ then ______________________

If ______________________ then ______________________

If ______________________ then ______________________

Tools / software used: ______________________

Templates / forms / scripts: ______________________

How do we know it's complete? ______________________

How is completion tracked? ______________________

Opportunities to Streamline

(connect with other Objectives)

____

____

____

____

____

____

This process is stored ______________________

Process owner: ______________________

Two-week check-in date: ______________________

product
your service

I KNOW THAT "product" might sound a bit weird when what we're talking about is legal services. And, no, I didn't name this pillar "Product" just because I needed another P to land the alliteration. (Although I must admit, it is quite handy.) My hope is that calling our lawyering "Product" will remind us to approach the services we deliver to our clients systematically—with frameworks and intentional design.

Without that, we end up serving inconsistently. One client gets our full attention and brilliant strategy. Another gets whoever's available and whatever approach feels right that day. The team still works hard but without a shared picture of what excellent service truly looks like. It's like cooking without a recipe every single time.

And I'm not talking about treating clients like customers at a drive-thru or churning cases through an assembly line. I'm talking about frameworks that ensure every client gets your best thinking. Tools that help them understand their situation. Systems that deliver consistent care whether you're in the room or not.

The foundation of Product is simple: Choose the right cases, understand what truly matters to your clients, and make sure your team approaches every case with the same level of excellence. These three elements work together.

When you're selective about cases (Product Exercise 1), you protect your capacity to truly understand each client's *why* (Product Exercise 2). When you understand their why, your strategic approach becomes more focused and meaningful (Product Exercise 3). And when your team has a consistent strategic framework, you can confidently take on clients, knowing you'll serve them well. Each piece supports the others, creating a Product pillar that's stronger than the sum of its parts. That's how you create consistency, protect your resources, and give every client the benefit of your best work.

Need a Refresher?

Go back to *The Set-Up*:

Chapter 11: It's All About the Client, if you need a reminder of why psychological safety matters and how to uncover your client's why through their mission and vision. Without safety, people hold back. With it, they share openly, and that's when you truly understand what matters most to them.

Chapter 12: A Better Way to Serve, if you need a reminder of how building strategic frameworks transforms service from inconsistent to reliable. This is where you stop reinventing the wheel and start delivering intentionally to every client, every time.

Product Exercise 1. Define Your Case Selection Criteria

Just because you can take a case doesn't mean you should. You don't have unlimited resources, and saying yes to everything that walks through the door isn't a strategy. It's how you burn out your team and fill your Pipeline with cases you regret.

Clear boundaries make decisions easier. When everyone knows what fits and what doesn't, your team can handle Intake confidently without needing your input on every potential file. This tool helps you define those boundaries so Intake runs smoother and you work on cases that move your firm forward.

Step 1: Define Your "Clear Yes" Cases

List the types of cases that are no-brainers for your firm. The ones you'll automatically accept:

1 ______________________________

2 ______________________________

3 ______________________________

Step 2: Describe Your Ideal Client

Who do you serve best (demographics, situation, mindset)?

____

____

____

____

____

____

____

Step 3: Set Your Value/Complexity Thresholds

What makes a case worth your time?

Minimum case value: $ ______________________________

Complexity level: ______________________________
(e.g., straightforward only, moderate complexity okay, complex cases welcomed)

Time investment: ______________________________
(e.g., max. six months from Intake to resolution, cases under 100 hours total)

Step 4: Identify Outliers Needing Attorney Review

What situations require attorney's input before being accepted?

1 ______________________________

2 ______________________________

3 ______________________________

Step 5: Plan Your "No" Process

For cases you don't take:

☐ Refer to specific firms (list two or three trusted referral partners)

☐ Decline outright with explanation

☐ Other:

Step 6: Train Your Team

Who handles Intake decisions?

____

____

When do they escalate to you?

____

____

____

____

____

____

Step 7: Document and Implement

Now, turn this into a working tool.

- ☐ Add your criteria to your Intake form or CMS so the team can reference it during calls.
- ☐ Schedule a team meeting to walk through these criteria and answer questions.
- ☐ Create a simple one-page reference sheet for your Intake team to keep at their desks.
- ☐ Set a 30-day check-in to review how it's working and adjust as needed.

Add any actions and related deadlines to your Set-Up Quarterly Plan. Also, include where your Case Selection Criteria is stored in your Set-Up Annual Plan so your team can find them.

Product Exercise 2. Identify Your Client's Why

When clients walk into your office, they're carrying more than just a legal problem. They're stepping into a world they may never have entered before, uncertain about the process, unsure of what to say, and cautious about whether they'll be heard. Most won't share what's really driving them unless they feel safe enough to be vulnerable. They need to know they're in a judgment-free space where their fears and hopes can be heard without criticism. They need to feel that you're listening and not just gathering facts to build a case.

This exercise is designed to help you create that safety. When clients feel genuinely heard and understood, they'll share the deeper story, one you can use to shape how you should handle their case. Finding their true why allows you to focus on what matters most, speak to their real concerns, and pursue outcomes that serve their true needs.

The questions in this exercise are designed to build that safety and trust through active listening. Active listening means reflecting back what you hear ("It sounds like you're worried about..."), asking follow-up questions that dig deeper ("Tell me more about that"), and creating pauses where clients can think and feel without rushing to fill the silence. When you listen this way, clients recognize they're being truly heard—often for the first time since their problem began. That recognition opens the door to honest conversation about what they really need.

The key is creating space for these deeper conversations early in the relationship. Spend an extra five minutes during Intake really listening to what's driving them. That investment shapes every decision that follows.

Step 1: Discover Your Client's Mission

These questions help you move past the surface issue to understand what's really at stake for your client right now.

- What has been the hardest part of this situation for you?
- What led you to decide to seek help now?
- How has this issue impacted your daily life or routine?
- What worries you most about how this could turn out?
- What would resolving this issue mean for you right now?
- What do you need most from us at this moment?

- What else about this situation is weighing on you?
- If you could resolve one thing immediately, what would that be?
- How would you describe the ideal outcome for your situation right now?

Step 2: Uncover Your Client's Vision

These questions reveal what your client hopes for beyond the immediate legal resolution.

- What do you want your life to look like after this is over?
- How do you see this impacting you or others in the future?
- What would a successful outcome mean for you in the long run?
- Is there a lasting change you hope this legal action can bring?
- What personal goals or values are most important to you in this situation?
- What's your ideal scenario once this case is resolved?
- Beyond this case, what broader change do you hope to see?

Step 3: Practice Uncovering Their Why

Choose a current client and practice uncovering their why, using the prompts above.

Client: ______________________________

Their stated legal issue:

____

____

____

____

____

____

Their mission (what they need right now):

Their vision (what they hope for in the long term):

Step 4: Brainstorm Ways to Apply Your Client's Why

Now that you understand how a client's mission and vision can reshape your approach, brainstorm specific ways to use these in your practice.

How could you reference their why in client communications?

How could their why influence your case strategy decisions?

What tools or processes could you create to keep their why visible throughout the duration of the case?

Next Step: Choose one idea above and implement it this week. *Add it to your Set-Up Quarterly Plan, with a specific deadline.*

Product Exercise 3. Build Your Team's Case Approach

Every case deserves the same level of strategic thinking, no matter who handles it or what type it is. The solution is systematizing the questions that lead to strategic breakthroughs. When everyone starts with the same analytical foundation, they can spend their creative energy on solving the case instead of figuring out how to approach it. Your firm's best practices become the standard everyone follows.

Step 1: Spot Inconsistencies

Think about your recent cases. Where does inconsistency show up in your team's approach?

Check the issues that sound familiar:

- ☐ Different team members focus on different things first (liability vs. damages vs. procedure)
- ☐ Strategic analysis happens too late in the process
- ☐ Strong cases get overlooked because the initial assessment is weak
- ☐ Team members miss key legal theories or defenses
- ☐ Client goals get lost in legal technicalities
- ☐ Case strategy varies wildly depending on who's handling it

Step 2: Capture Your Best Practices

A strong strategy always starts with strong questions. When your team begins every case with the same key questions, they anchor their analysis in what works instead of drifting in different directions. The questions create a shared foundation, so your team spends less time figuring out where to begin and more time building a winning strategy.

Think about your strongest cases, the ones where strategy clicked early. What questions helped you spot the path forward? What questions did you ask that led to the breakthrough? (For reference, you can see how we systematized our strategic thinking with the Case Narrative [the case strategy we start building on day one and refine throughout the case] and the Bad Faith Triangle [our way of engaging our clients with the legal aspects of their cases] in chapter 12 of *The Set-Up*.)

Write down five to seven questions your team should always ask at the start of a case. For example:

- What facts strengthen or weaken liability?
- Where are the likely damages, and how do we prove them?
- What defenses is the other side most likely to raise?
- What procedural hurdles could slow us down?
- What is the client's real goal beyond "winning"?

1 ______________________________

2 ______________________________

3 ______________________________

4 ______________________________

5 ______________________________

6 ______________________________

7 ______________________________

Step 3: Test and Make It Standard

Use your questions on a current case. Do they spark strategic thinking? Refine if needed, then train your team to use this approach on every new case.

Remember: Product thinking isn't a one-time project. It's the habit of turning your best instincts into repeatable systems that serve every client, every time. Start your next new case with the questions you created in Step 2 this week and watch how it changes your team's approach.

Step 4: Implement Your Framework

☐ **Document your approach:** How will you capture this? (template, one-pager, case file checklist, etc.)

____

____

____

☐ **Train your team:** When and how? (team meeting date, practice session, case walk-throughs, etc.)

☐ **Make it standard:** How will you ensure it's used consistently? (required at Intake, built into CMS, monthly audits, etc.)

Add your framework rollout to your Set-Up Quarterly Plan. Include your training date, who's responsible for ensuring the questions are used, and your 30-day check-in to assess adoption.

profitability
your results

FOR MOST FIRM OWNERS, money feels less like something steady and more like a roller coaster: thrilling on the way up, terrifying on the way down, and exhausting in between. That ride comes with a pit in your stomach when settlements or client payments are delayed and payroll is due. The 3:00 a.m. math problem you never signed up for: *Will this month's income stretch far enough?* The feast-and-famine cycle that makes every decision feel like a gamble.

You might have a bookkeeper for the day-to-day or an accountant for compliance. That's valuable support. But the bigger choices—how your firm allocates its money—still land on your desk. And those choices aren't optional. Profitability isn't the extra you hope for at the end of the month; it's part of the foundation your firm stands on. When your money has clear pathways, defined purposes, and predictable patterns, you stop reacting to financial surprises and start preventing them. You make decisions from clarity instead of fear.

In the next few pages, you'll find some simple tools: an honest snapshot of where your money's going, a plan for what happens when money comes in, and guidance on using your Pipeline dashboard to forecast cash flow before problems hit. Then you'll choose what to measure to confirm your Set-Up is delivering results.

Need a Refresher?

Go back to *The Set-Up*:

Chapter 13: Investing in People, if you need a reminder on why supporting your team is one of the smartest profitability strategies you'll ever use.

Chapter 14: Measure It and It Will Come, if you need a reminder on how KPIs cut through the noise and show you where your firm is thriving (and where it's stalling).

Chapter 15: Mastering the Money, if you need a reminder of the Profit First approach and how to finally give every dollar a job so you can breathe easier.

Profitability Exercise 1. Know Your Numbers

Before you can build sustainable profitability, you need to know three basic pieces of information. Think of these as your financial vital signs. They're simple numbers that tell you if your firm is healthy or struggling.

Step 1: Know Your Monthly Break-Even Number

This is the minimum amount your firm needs to bring in each month just to keep the doors open. This is your floor. Any month you don't hit this number, you're going backward.

Add up what you pay every month, no matter what:

Rent: $ ______________________________

Payroll (including your pay): $ ______________________________

Insurance: $ ______________________________

Basic software: $ ______________________________

Other monthly expenses
(utilities, phone, marketing, bar dues, etc.): $ ______________________________

Your break-even number: $ ______________________________

This is your minimum monthly target. Every case you consider should be evaluated against this: Will this case help me hit break-even consistently?

Step 2: Know Your Legal Fee Income (LFI) Pattern

Track your legal fee income (LFI) over the last six months. LFI is the money the firm has earned, including fees billed and collected, your portion of settlement proceeds, and retainers. Don't count client's money passing through trust accounts or cost reimbursements.

Month 1: $ __________ Month 2: $ __________ Month 3: $ __________

Month 4: $ __________ Month 5: $ __________ Month 6: $ __________

Your highest month: $ ____________________

Your lowest month: $ ____________________

Income gap (highest minus lowest): $ ____________________

Average monthly LFI: $ ____________________
(add the numbers for six months above and divide by six)

Now compare your income to your break-even:

Is your *average* LFI above your break-even? ☐ Yes ☐ No

Is your *lowest* month above your break-even? ☐ Yes ☐ No

Income gap (highest minus lowest): $ ____________________

What this tells you:

- If your average is below break-even, you're not bringing in enough work.
- If your lowest month is below break-even, you have a cash flow problem—some months you can't cover basics.
- If your income gap is more than 50 percent of your average monthly LFI, your income is unpredictable. (This is especially common in contingency practices.) It makes planning much more difficult, but at least now you can see the pattern and work with it.

Step 3: Know Your Owner's Compensation Reality

If you're not paying yourself (and your partners, if you have them) consistently, or if what you're paying isn't enough, your firm isn't profitable yet—no matter what the bank balance says.

Do you pay yourself consistently?

- ☐ Yes, same amount every month
- ☐ Sometimes, when there's extra money
- ☐ Rarely or never

Current monthly owner's compensation: $ ____________________

Owner's compensation target
(what you need to cover personal expenses): $ ____________________

Monthly shortfall (if any): $ ____________________
(To calculate: owner's compensation target minus current owner's compensation)

Step 4: Record Your Baseline Numbers

You now have your three must-have numbers. These show you exactly where your firm stands financially.

Break-even: $ ____________________

Average monthly LFI: $ ____________________

Owner's compensation target: $ ____________________

Write these down in your Set-Up Quarterly Plan and check them monthly during your Set-Up Time.

Profitability Exercise 2. Give Every Dollar a Job

Now that you know your baseline numbers, it's time to fix the biggest problem most law firms face: money coming in without a plan for where it goes. You've seen the cycle. Revenue hits your account, you pay the urgent bills, cover payroll, and handle whatever's screaming the loudest. At the end of the month, you look at what's left and hope there's something for you and maybe something to set aside for future growth. But "whatever's left" isn't a business strategy. It's wishful thinking.

What if every dollar had a specific job before it ever hit your main account? What if profit wasn't what remained after spending, but what got protected first? That's the shift I first learned from Mike Michalowicz in his book *Profit First: Transform Your Business from a Cash-Eating Monster to a Money-Making Machine*. His approach completely reframed the way I thought about cash flow and gave me the foundation to create a version tailored for law firms.

Step 1: Set Up Multiple Accounts

Create separate accounts that each have a specific job. (If your banker or accountant balks at this, tell them you're doing the Profit First system and refer them to Mike Michalowicz's excellent book.) How many accounts you need depends on how you get paid.

Accounts for hourly/flat-fee firms:

- **Profit:** money that stays in the business for growth, emergencies, and building reserves
- **Tax:** quarterly tax payments
- **Owner's Compensation:** your salary
- **Operating:** day-to-day expenses: rent, staff payroll, insurance, software, utilities, and other monthly costs

Accounts for contingency firms:

(same as above, but add two more)

- **Trust:** client settlements (IOLTA compliance)
- **Case Expenses:** money you use to advance case costs to clients (medical records, filing fees, expert witnesses, etc.). This account tracks what clients owe you back when their case settles.

Step 2: Assign Your Starting Percentages

Based on your owner's compensation shortfall and LFI pattern from Exercise 1, set your starting percentages for each account.

If you have a volume problem (average LFI below break-even), start conservatively:

- Profit: 1 percent
- Tax: 10 percent
- Owner's Compensation: Whatever covers your minimum personal needs
- Operating: Everything left over

If you have a consistency problem (volatile LFI but hitting break-even on average), you can be slightly more aggressive:

- Profit: 3 percent
- Tax: 10 percent
- Owner's Compensation: What you need to live comfortably
- Operating: Everything left over

Start small on profit to build the habit of always allocating to that account. You'll feel the impact after your very first allocation. Increase it by 1 percent each quarter as the system takes hold, working toward 10 percent profit as your target.

Starting allocation percentages:

Profit: ________ %

Tax: ________ %

Owner's Compensation: ________ %

Operating: ________ % (whatever's left)

For Hourly/Flat-Fee Firms: Every time revenue comes in, immediately move your profit, owner's compensation, and tax percentages. Leave everything else in the operating account for expenses.

For Contingency Firms: First, set up your case expenses account. Decide how much you typically have outstanding in case costs at any given time and fund your case expenses account with that amount. (Transfer it from the operating account as a one-time set-up.)

Starting case expenses balance: $ __________ (If the operating account doesn't have this amount, start with what you can and build it up over the next few months as money comes in.)

From now on:

- Pay case costs directly from this account.
- When settlements come in, reimburse this account for costs advanced.

This keeps your case expenses visible as assets (money clients owe you) rather than buried in the operating account.

When a settlement comes in:

- Move all funds to trust first.
- Pay the client their portion.
- Reimburse case expenses to the case expenses account (to replenish what you advanced).
- Allocate your LFI to profit, owner's compensation, and tax accounts at their assigned percentages and put the remainder into the operating account.

Step 3: Check In Monthly

Every month, review your allocation.

Is the operating account running too tight?

- ☐ Yes, reduce other percentages temporarily
- ☐ No, consider raising profit account percentage

Are you consistently hitting your owner's compensation target?

- ☐ Yes, you're paying yourself like you matter
- ☐ No, adjust percentages or cut operating expenses

Is the tax account building appropriately?

- ☐ Yes, no surprises at tax time
- ☐ No, increase percentage or check with your accountant

Has profit grown since you started?

- ☐ Yes, increase the percentage in the account
- ☐ No, look at operating expenses or revenue

The Safety Rules

Cash flow crunches happen, but you still need guardrails to protect what matters most. That's where the safety rules come in. Never borrow from

- trust (illegal),
- tax (painful),
- or profit (defeats the purpose).

If you absolutely must, you can borrow from owner's compensation or operating account—but only if you pay it back as soon as new revenue comes in. And if the operating account is empty, the rule is simple: The answer is no until more money arrives.

Document your allocation percentages in your Set-Up Annual Plan and your monthly review schedule in your Set-Up Quarterly Plan.

Profitability Exercise 3. Track What Matters

You can't manage what you don't measure. But most law firms either measure nothing or try to measure everything. Neither works.

Key performance indicators (KPIs) are a handful of metrics that tell you how your firm is doing and, if you're struggling, what needs attention. Think of them as an early warning system, showing you what's going wrong before it becomes expensive to fix.

When starting with KPIs, pick one metric that will have the biggest impact on your biggest problem. Master that before adding others. Choose something your actions can change. You can't control when judges make decisions, but you can control how quickly you respond to discovery. Put it somewhere you'll review regularly. If it's buried in a spreadsheet you never open, it won't drive behavior.

You'll know your KPI is working when your team pays attention to it without prompting, issues get spotted and fixed early, and the number keeps moving in the direction you want.

Remember: Missing your KPI target isn't failure; it's information. The whole point is to see what's really happening so you can adjust before small problems become big ones.

KPIs Made Simple

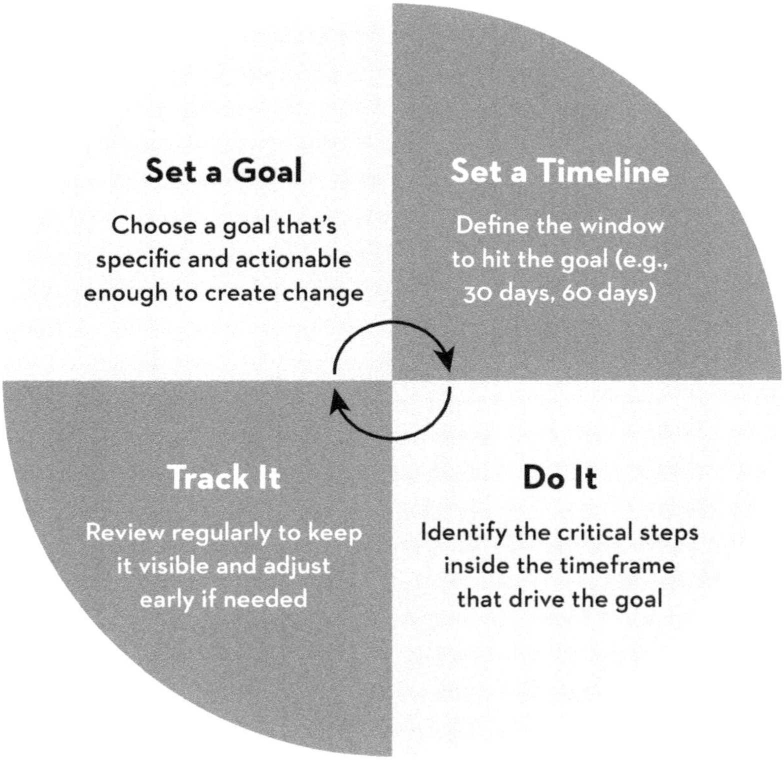

KPIs follow a simple four-step pattern:

1. **Set a goal:** Choose something specific that will move your firm forward.
2. **Set a timeline:** Give it a window to happen in.
3. **Do it:** Identify critical steps that drive the goal.
4. **Track it:** Review it regularly and adjust when needed.

KPI Examples by Pillar

people

Read one professional development book per quarter.

Conduct monthly value check-ins.

pipeline

Send demand letters within 60 days of client finishing treatment.

Move cases from Intake to Stage One within 30 days.

process

Implement two workflow improvements per quarter.

Have backup coverage for every critical process.

product

Complete client *why* discovery within first week.

Achieve policy limits offers on 70% of appropriate cases.

profitability

Increase profit allocation percentage by 1% each quarter.

Keep collection time under 45 days.

These are examples to spark ideas. Choose KPIs that address your firm's specific challenges.

Step 1: Build Your First KPI

Choose your pillar (pick where you feel the most pain right now):

☐ People ☐ Pipeline ☐ Process ☐ Product ☐ Profitability

1. Set a Goal

(Make it specific and actionable.)

2. Set a Timeline

(Give it a realistic window.)

3. Do It

(What critical steps drive this goal?)

____

____

____

____

____

____

____

4. Track It

Review schedule: ☐ Weekly ☐ Monthly ☐ Other: __________

Current status: ______________________________

Next action: ______________________________

Next review date: ______________________________

Now Make It Real

1. Put your review date on your calendar right now.
2. Add this KPI and review schedule to your Set-Up Quarterly Plan.
3. After 90 days of tracking one KPI successfully, consider adding a second one.

Remember: One KPI tracked consistently beats five tracked sporadically. Start small, build the habit, then expand.

Fix It

WHEN SOMETHING goes wrong in your firm, it's easy to reach for what seems an obvious fix. Cash flow dips, so you think you need to market more. A case stalls, so you assign it to someone else. A paralegal seems overwhelmed, so you go hire another one. It feels like it's what you're supposed to do, but often you're just applying expensive Band-Aids to problems you haven't bothered to understand. No offense intended here, but marketing won't help if your Pipeline leaks. A new hire won't solve role confusion. Working longer hours won't fix undercharging.

This issue makes me think of my friend Laura. Laura's an ophthalmologist who hit a wall in her late thirties—exhausted, struggling, and told she was "fine" by doctors who only looked at symptoms. The search for real answers led her to functional medicine, which asks "why" instead of just treating what hurts, looking at the whole bodily system, not just the symptoms. When Laura was later diagnosed with breast cancer, she understood it wasn't an isolated event—it was the loudest signal from a body that had been whispering for years.

Law firms show symptoms, too. Files pile up. Decisions stall. Energy spikes and crashes. The instinct is the same: Patch it quick. But short-term fixes don't solve long-term problems.

Before you reach for another tactic, slow down and ask: What's really going on here? The tools in this chapter will help you diagnose what's under the surface so you can fix the problem at its root. Use them anytime your firm feels off track. They'll serve you again and again as your firm grows and shifts.

Need a Refresher?

Go back to *The Set-Up*:

Chapter 16: Beyond the Sum of Its Parts, if you need a reminder on how to diagnose the real issue (not just the symptom), filter opportunities through the five pillars before saying yes, and see how The Set-Up scales as you grow.

Fix It Exercise 1. The Root Cause Detective Tool

Like functional medicine for your firm, the Root Cause Detective Tool helps you trace symptoms back to their source. Use it during your Set-Up Time when you can think strategically, not reactively. Return to it whenever something feels off.

Step 1: Name the Symptom

What's the issue you're trying to solve? Be specific. Think in terms of what you're seeing, hearing, or feeling. Examples:

- "Cases are stalling after Intake."
- "Team keeps asking me the same questions."
- "Cash flow is too unpredictable."
- "Client updates are falling through the cracks."
- "I'm constantly in firefighting mode."

Your symptom:

____

____

____

____

The Root Cause Detective Tool

DIAGNOSIS

1. **Name the Symptom**
What's the issue you're seeing, hearing, or feeling?

↓

2. **Pattern or One-Off?**
Has this happened before?
Patterns = structural issues.

↓

3. **Follow Symptom to Source**
Consider each pillar: Could this be where your symptom is rooted? Which one feels most connected to the symptom?

↓

4. **Ask Why Three Times**
Keep digging until you uncover the root cause, not just the surface symptom.

TREATMENT

↓

5. **Decide What Needs Fixing**
Identify the action that addresses the root cause and strengthens your system.

↓

6. **Add to Set-Up Plan**
Document, assign ownership, and follow up as progress is made.

Stop treating symptoms. Fix the system.

Step 2: Ask "Is This a Pattern or a One-Off?"

Look for history. Has this happened before? How often? What did you do last time?

- ☐ This is a one-off (first time or rare occurrence). → A quick fix might be enough. Handle it and move on.
- ☐ This is a pattern (happened multiple times). → Stop patching. Repeated problems mean something structural is broken. If you keep applying bandages, the symptom will keep showing up—maybe in a different form, maybe with a different person, but it will come back.

If you checked "This is a pattern," commit to finding the root cause in Steps 3 and 4.

Notes:

____

____

____

____

____

Step 3: Follow the Symptom to the Source

For each pillar, consider: Could this be where my symptom is rooted?

People: Could this be about who's doing the work, how they're led, or whether they're aligned with our mission?

____

____

____

____

Pipeline: Could this be about unclear stages or roles, missing handoffs, or nobody knowing what happens next?

Process: Could this be about how work gets done—or doesn't get done—consistently?

Product: Could this be about taking the wrong cases, inconsistent service, or unclear standards?

Profitability: Could this be about money—pricing, staffing, resources, or not tracking what matters?

Which pillar feels most connected to your symptom? ______

Step 4: Ask Why Three Times

Just like a doctor—or a good cross-examiner—get curious. Each answer leads to another layer. Keep asking why until you uncover the root cause.

See the graphic below for examples across all five pillars.

people

SYMPTOM: **"Team feels disconnected, going through the motions"**

▼

No one remembers why this work matters

▼

Haven't discussed mission or values in months

▼

Too focused on operations, stopped reinforcing culture

ROOT CAUSE: **Values not actively reinforced**

pipeline

SYMPTOM: **"Cases are stalling after intake"**

▼

Team isn't sure what to do next

▼

No clear intake-to-case-start handoff defined

▼

Never defined stages or responsibilities after Intake

ROOT CAUSE: **Missing Pipeline structure**

process

SYMPTOM: **"Team keeps asking me the same questions"**

▼

Everyone does the task differently

▼

No documented process for key workflows

▼

Assumed everyone knew how to do it

ROOT CAUSE: **Processes not documented**

product

SYMPTOM: **"Team scrambles at deposition and trial prep"**

▼

Strategy isn't clear until late in the case

▼

Working reactively instead of strategically

▼

No framework for thinking through cases from day one

ROOT CAUSE: **No strategic case-building framework**

profitability

SYMPTOM: **"Cash flow is too unpredictable"**

▼

Money comes in, but not sure where it goes

▼

Don't allocate fund to specific purposes

▼

Never set up a system for managing profit and expenses

ROOT CAUSE: **No system for money allocation**

Now try it with your symptom.

1. Why? ____________________

2. Why? ____________________

3. Why? ____________________

What root cause did you uncover?

____

____

____

Step 5: Decide What Needs Fixing

Now that you've identified the likely cause, what action will address it? For example:

- Create a handoff checklist for Intake to litigation.
- Define who owns each step of Stage Two.
- Document your records request process.
- Review and clarify your pricing model.
- Schedule a weekly team debrief to catch patterns early.

Your Fix It focus:

____

____

____

Step 6: Add to Set-Up Plan

Document your Fix It focus as an action in your Set-Up Quarterly Plan, assign ownership, and follow up as progress is made.

Fix It Exercise 2. The Interconnection Check

Once you've identified your root cause, don't stop there. Problems in law firms rarely travel alone—they create ripple effects across multiple pillars.

Cases stall at every handoff (Pipeline) because of unclear leadership (People)—no one knows who decides what. The stalled cases force everyone to improvise constantly (Process), which creates wildly different client experiences, depending on who handles the file (Product). Inconsistent service leads to unpredictable settlements and fee collections (Profitability), which creates financial stress that makes you reactive and short-tempered as a leader (back to People).

The cycle feeds itself.

And the beauty is that, due to the interconnected nature of the pillars, one fix can solve multiple problems. Understanding these connections helps you predict—and maximize—the impact of addressing your root cause.

Step 1: Map the Connections

Consider how your root cause from Fix It Exercise 1 might be creating problems in other pillars. If a connection isn't obvious, that's okay; just leave it blank. The goal is to spot the ones that exist.

People: How is this root cause affecting your team's morale, clarity, or ability to do their work?

____

____

____

Pipeline: How is this root cause creating bottlenecks or delays?

____

____

____

Process: How is this root cause forcing workarounds, inconsistency, or wasted time?

Product: How is this root cause affecting client experience, service quality, or case outcomes?

Profitability: How is this root cause impacting cash flow, expenses, or your ability to plan financially?

Step 2: Count the Impact

How many pillars are affected by your root cause? (Count how many you filled in above.)

Three-plus pillars affected? Your root cause fix will create cascading improvements across your firm. This is high-leverage work—prioritize it.

One–two pillars affected? Your fix is still valuable but more contained. Handle it, but don't expect firm-wide transformation.

In your Set-Up Quarterly or Annual Plan, note which pillars will improve when you address the root cause. This helps you track the full impact of your work. Now that you know what needs fixing, Exercise 3 will help you make sure you fix it the right way. That means structurally, not just tactically.

Fix It Exercise 3. Structural Fixes vs. Tactical Patches

Everywhere you look, someone's selling "the thing" that will transform your firm. The new CMS. The marketing system. The productivity hack. The hiring strategy. And, yes, some of these tools are genuinely useful—but only if you have the foundation to support them. Without that foundation, even good tactics fail. You implement the new system, but your team doesn't use it because Roles aren't clear. You launch the marketing campaign, but leads get stuck because your Pipeline leaks. You hire great people, but they burn out because your processes force them to reinvent everything. It's like trying to invite guests over when you haven't built the house yet. Build the house first. Then worry about the furniture.

So, every time you're about to implement a fix, ask yourself: Is this fix about getting through today (tactical) or building something that will still work a year from now (foundational)?

Tactical Patch Solves today's problem		**Structural Fix** Builds something lasting
Hiring someone to handle more work when things get crazy busy	→	Hiring someone who fits your culture and strengthens your team
Jumping in to fix a problem yourself (again)	→	Training your team so they know how to solve the problem next time
Scrambling to cover bills while waiting on the next big fee	→	Building a money system that puts you in control
Adding new software to "fix" communication issues	→	Creating clear Pipeline stages so everyone knows what comes next

The Root Cause Detective Tool you used in Fix It Exercise 1 has pointed you toward one of the five pillars: People, Pipeline, Process, Product, or Profitability. That's your foundation. Now make sure your solution strengthens that pillar rather than just patching the symptom.

Answer this: How will this fix still be working a year from now?

If you don't see how it will be working a year from now, you're probably applying a tactic to a structural problem. Focus on the foundation first. Then the tactics will stick.

When Tactics Do Make Sense

Tactics only work when your foundation is solid. If you haven't addressed the structural issues identified in Exercise 1, adding tactics is like hanging pictures on a crumbling wall. They won't fix what's broken. Instead, they'll just give you more to manage.

But once you've addressed the structural issue, tactics can provide powerful support. They strengthen a pillar that's already standing and make day-to-day life easier.

Before implementing any of these tactics, ask yourself: Have I addressed the root cause in this pillar? If yes, proceed. If no, go back to Fix It Exercise 1.

If your structure is sound and you want to shore it up, scan the list below for practical options.

People

- Hire with values, not just résumés
- Embed values in performance reviews
- Hold Monday Morning Meetings focused on growth and values
- Celebrate Values in Action wins weekly
- Use value-based performance improvement plans

Pipeline

- Hold daily or weekly huddles to spot bottlenecks
- Run a whiteboard exercise where everyone shows their Role and Objectives
- Share a one-page Pipeline snapshot with clients
- Run quarterly Pipeline reviews with your team
- Run a stalled-case sweep each week to clear bottlenecks

Process

- Standardize email templates for routine client updates
- Write down your top five recurring workflows
- Implement "if/then" rules for recurring problems (e.g., missed client calls)
- Create cross-training routines so coverage is never a scramble
- Conduct a quarterly Process audit, where the team picks one–two clunky steps to streamline

Product

- Create plain-language client guides (discovery, mediation, trial)
- Develop checklists for common case types
- Build Intake scripts to uncover the client's why
- Offer follow-up calls after case closure to reinforce client care
- Record short video explainers (two–three minutes) to clarify common questions

Profitability

- Review fee agreements for clarity and enforceability
- Schedule monthly financial reviews (with your bookkeeper or alone)
- Build a small emergency reserve (even $5k–10k), if one doesn't exist
- Tighten case-expense reimbursement tracking
- Share financial snapshots with your team to build transparency

Pick one to two tactics that would strengthen your foundation. *Add them to your Set-Up Quarterly Plan.*

Make It Work

MY FRIEND AND WRITING COACH, author AJ Harper, once used a metaphor describing the author's journey as being like a six-lane highway. Some days you're focused on editing your book; others, you might be creating marketing pages or preparing a presentation. You have to do all of these things at the same time while progressing in each. I've adapted the metaphor for *The Set-Up* because it captures exactly how running a firm feels.

Each lane represents one of the five pillars—People, Pipeline, Process, Product, and Profitability—plus one lane for the "Fix It" chapter. Sometimes you need to put heavy focus on one lane—building your Pipeline from scratch or overhauling your money system—while the other lanes keep moving smoothly on their own. Other times you're in the "Fix It" lane, doing diagnostic work to figure out which pillar needs attention.

The Set-Up Plan is your traffic helicopter. It gives you a clear view of the lanes that are moving, the ones that need work, and the ones to focus your energy on so you can switch lanes strategically and keep the whole highway flowing smoothly. The Set-Up Plan has two parts.

The Set-Up Annual Plan gives you the big picture—your year-long vision for each pillar, reference for your foundational documents, and your overarching goals for the year. Fill this out once at the start of the year (or when you start *The Set-Up*) and return to it each quarter to stay aligned.

The Set-Up Quarterly Plan is where strategy meets action. Every ninety days, you'll identify your focus pillar, set your top priorities, assign owners and deadlines, track progress, and reflect on what's working. You'll decide on the focus pillar, which gets the most attention and action items, but you'll track progress across all five pillars—because even if you're focused on building your Pipeline, you might still be doing some People or Process work. Photocopy these pages or download them at theset-up.co/workbookresources—once each quarter—and keep all four with your annual plan. Together, these two plans give you altitude and traction—the vision and the vehicle for making your law firm run smoothly.

The plans are designed to work within your Set-Up Time. You'll check your progress, update your status, spot what's stalling, and plan your next move. And bring your team into this process. Shared ownership leads to shared success—and your Set-Up Plan becomes more powerful when everyone is invested in it.

When Plans Don't Go According to Plan

Finally, know that you likely won't hit every quarterly goal or target in your annual plan. That doesn't mean you're bad at planning or there's something wrong with your firm. Clients have emergencies. "Simple" processes reveal hidden complexities. This happens to every firm owner, including me.

When that happens, get curious instead of beating yourself up. Ask yourself: Was I aiming too high this time? Did urgent casework steal the time I meant for building systems? Did I hit a resource or knowledge gap I didn't see coming? Was this goal never as important as I thought it was?

Then decide what to do next. You can push a goal into the next quarter if it still matters and you've made some progress. Shrink it if the scope was too big but part of it might still make a difference. Swap it out if something more urgent deserves the spot. Or just let it go completely if it's not critical right now. That's not quitting. It's being smart about priorities. Because missing a goal doesn't wreck the plan unless you let it. The only thing that matters is whether you're making progress. Two goals finished well will always beat three goals half-baked.

Then, next quarter, give yourself a little more margin. Set one fewer goal or several smaller ones. Write down what you didn't complete and why. Over time, you'll start spotting your own patterns. That's how planning gets easier and your progress becomes more achievable over time.

And remember, your Systems Check scores will show you the real story. Even when individual goals are missed, if your pillar scores are climbing, you're winning.

The Set-Up Annual Plan | Year: ____________

Your year-long vision for strengthening your firm's foundation.

Our Foundation (Reference Documents)

Mission & Core Values stored at ____________________________

Pipeline Structure stored at ____________________________

Process Capture Sheets stored at ____________________________

Case Selection Criteria stored at ____________________________

Product Frameworks stored at ____________________________

Profitability Baseline Numbers

Monthly Break-Even: $____________________________

Average Monthly LFI: $____________________________

Owner's Compensation Target: $____________________________

Systems Check Score Tracking

Quarter	People	Pipeline	Process	Product	Profitability
Q1					
Q2					
Q3					
Q4					

Annual Plan by Pillar

People

This year, we will:

Pipeline

This year, we will:

Process

This year, we will:

Product

This year, we will:

Profitability

This year, we will:

Annual Aim

By year-end, we will have accomplished:

Five-Year Vision

When we look back in five years, we want to say:

The Set-Up Quarterly Plan | Q ________ Year: ________

Your focus for this quarter. Review at 30/60/90 days.

Date Started: ________

30-Day Check-In: ________

60-Day Check-In: ________

90-Day Check-In: ________

Systems Check Scores This Quarter

People	Pipeline	Process	Product	Profitability

Focus Pillar This Quarter: ________ (lowest score from Systems Check)

My Top 3 Priorities This Quarter: (These can span multiple pillars—your biggest-impact work)

1 ________

2 ________

3 ________

People

This Quarter's Focus:

____

____

My KPI or Specific Goal:

____

____

Target: __________ | Timeline: __________ | Owner: __________

My To-Dos:

1 ______________________________

Owner: __________ | Deadline: __________
Status: ☐ Not Started ☐ In Progress ☐ Complete

2 ______________________________

Owner: __________ | Deadline: __________
Status: ☐ Not Started ☐ In Progress ☐ Complete

3 ______________________________

Owner: __________ | Deadline: __________
Status: ☐ Not Started ☐ In Progress ☐ Complete

Progress Tracking:

30 Days: ______________________________

60 Days: ______________________________

90 Days: ______________________________

Pipeline

This Quarter's Focus:

____

____

My KPI or Specific Goal:

____

____

Target: ____________ | Timeline: ____________ | Owner: ____________

My To-Dos:

1 ____

Owner: ____________ | Deadline: ____________
Status: ☐ Not Started ☐ In Progress ☐ Complete

2 ____

Owner: ____________ | Deadline: ____________
Status: ☐ Not Started ☐ In Progress ☐ Complete

3 ____

Owner: ____________ | Deadline: ____________
Status: ☐ Not Started ☐ In Progress ☐ Complete

Progress Tracking:

30 Days: ____

60 Days: ____

90 Days: ____

Process

This Quarter's Focus:

____

____

My KPI or Specific Goal:

____

____

Target: ____________ | Timeline: ____________ | Owner: ____________

My To-Dos:

1 ____

Owner: ________________ | Deadline: ________________

Status: ☐ Not Started ☐ In Progress ☐ Complete

2 ____

Owner: ________________ | Deadline: ________________

Status: ☐ Not Started ☐ In Progress ☐ Complete

3 ____

Owner: ________________ | Deadline: ________________

Status: ☐ Not Started ☐ In Progress ☐ Complete

Progress Tracking:

30 Days: ____________________________________

60 Days: ____________________________________

90 Days: ____________________________________

Product

This Quarter's Focus:

____

____

My KPI or Specific Goal:

____

____

Target: __________ | Timeline: __________ | Owner: __________

My To-Dos:

1 ______________________________________

Owner: __________ | Deadline: __________
Status: ☐ Not Started ☐ In Progress ☐ Complete

2 ______________________________________

Owner: __________ | Deadline: __________
Status: ☐ Not Started ☐ In Progress ☐ Complete

3 ______________________________________

Owner: __________ | Deadline: __________
Status: ☐ Not Started ☐ In Progress ☐ Complete

Progress Tracking:

30 Days: __________________________________

60 Days: __________________________________

90 Days: __________________________________

Profitability

This Quarter's Focus:

____

____

My KPI or Specific Goal:

____

____

Target: ______________ | Timeline: ______________ | Owner: ______________

My To-Dos:

1 ____

Owner: ______________ | Deadline: ______________

Status: ☐ Not Started ☐ In Progress ☐ Complete

2 ____

Owner: ______________ | Deadline: ______________

Status: ☐ Not Started ☐ In Progress ☐ Complete

3 ____

Owner: ______________ | Deadline: ______________

Status: ☐ Not Started ☐ In Progress ☐ Complete

Progress Tracking:

30 Days: ____

60 Days: ____

90 Days: ____

Quarterly Reflection

What worked well:

What needs adjustment:

Biggest wins this quarter:

Focus pillar for next quarter (based on current Systems Check):

Your New Normal

DO YOU REMEMBER that scene in *The Karate Kid* where Daniel finally loses it with Mr. Miyagi? He's been waxing cars and painting fences and sanding floors for weeks, and he's had enough. "When am I going to learn karate?" he demands, frustrated and ready to walk away. Then Mr. Miyagi tells him to show the motions. Wax on, wax off. Paint up, paint down. When Daniel does it, his arms move in perfect defensive blocks. All those chores he thought were meaningless were building muscle memory. He was training his body to respond without thinking.

I'm guessing you've had some version of that same moment while working through this workbook. Maybe you were knee-deep in Systems Checks or Pipeline mapping, wondering when you'd get to the "real" work of running your firm. Maybe the Process documentation felt like busy work, or you questioned whether all these exercises would change anything.

My hope is that you now understand you weren't just filling out worksheets. You were building something profound. You now have the discernment to know where to focus when everything feels urgent.

From here on out, when you sense a shift in your team's energy, you'll instinctively check your climate (People). When cases start moving slowly, you'll examine your Pipeline for bottlenecks without the old panic. When the same problems keep surfacing, you'll recognize it's a Process issue—not a character flaw in your team, not proof you're somehow failing.

The challenges won't disappear. Unfortunately, they never do. But now when opposing counsel plays dirty, when a key employee quits, or when cash flow tightens, your response will come from training, not terror. You'll know what to do because your instincts have been shaped by the work you've already done here.

The Set-Up was never meant to be a project you complete and shelve. It was meant to change how you think. And it has. You've learned to see your firm through its pillars. They're your muscle memory now, your automatic response to whatever walks through your door next. You've built the kind of firm you once only hoped for. Go back to page one and read what you wrote down as your why. You're living it now—your new normal.

Acknowledgments

MANY OF the same people who made *The Set-Up* possible guided this workbook, too, and I'm grateful beyond words.

To my team, my family, my publisher, and every firm owner committed to building better: Thank you for believing this work matters and that law firms can be different. That's exactly what makes it all worth doing.

SHEVAUN WILLIAMS

About the Author

SIMONE FULMER GAUS is co-founder of Fulmer Sill, a nationally recognized law firm based in Oklahoma City, focusing on personal injury, bad faith, and mass torts.

After seventeen years in practice, Simone was done with burnout and business as usual in the traditional law firm setting. She believed there had to be a better way to run a law firm—one that didn't cost your soul to succeed. So, in 2014, she started her own firm to find out if it was possible.

That journey led to The Set-Up™, a new model for running a law firm with more focus, more heart, and a lot less noise. In the eleven years since, her firm's revenue has grown more than thirteen times, proving that you can thrive in this business without sacrificing yourself or your team in the process.

Simone lives in Oklahoma City with her husband, Mark, in a house run by three Doodles and two Ragdolls. They share four grown kids and have recently stepped into their favorite role yet: grandparents.

What's Next?

Take a moment to look at how far you've come. You've brought structure, clarity, and calm to the work that once felt overwhelming. The next step? Keep going! Your firm will keep growing as you do.

Keep Building

If you haven't read the book yet, it's the perfect next step. *The Set-Up* gives you the strategy behind what you've been working through here and the deeper why behind each pillar. You'll also find more exercises and ideas in the book.

Find it wherever books are sold or order in bulk for your team at **theset-up.co.**

Want Extra Tools and Templates?

Not everything fit inside these pages. You'll find workbook-specific bonus exercises, examples, and downloadable resources at **theset-up.co/workbook resources.**

Need a Guide Along the Way?

I work directly with a small number of firm owners—leaders who want clarity, accountability, and a partner to help them strengthen every pillar of their firm—each year.

If that's you, let's talk.

Bring The Set-Up to Your Team or Event

I speak at CLEs, legal conferences, and team retreats about the following:

- building a value-driven culture
- creating accountability without burnout
- structure and systems that scale

Find details at **theset-up.co/speaking**.

Stay Connected

Join my email list for practical tools, new resources, and behind-the-scenes updates on upcoming programs.

Subscribe at **theset-up.co**.

Share Your Wins

If this workbook helped you bring order, accountability, and breathing room to your firm, please take a moment to leave a review online. Your feedback might be the encouragement another firm owner needs to finally build their foundation.

Thanks for trusting this process.

Here's to what you'll build next.

www.ingramcontent.com/pod-product-compliance
Ingram Content Group UK Ltd.
Pitfield, Milton Keynes, MK11 3LW, UK
UKHW062009041026
15591UKWH00017B/1253

9 781774 588031